on track ...

The Allman Brothers Band

every album, every song

Andrew Wild

sonicbondpublishing.com

Sonicbond Publishing Limited
www.sonicbondpublishing.co.uk
Email: info@sonicbondpublishing.co.uk

First Published in the United Kingdom 2022
First Published in the United States 2022

British Library Cataloguing in Publication Data:
A Catalogue record for this book is available from the British Library

Copyright Andrew Wild 2022

ISBN 978-1-78952-252-5

Typeset in ITC Garamond & ITC Avant Garde.
Printed and bound in England

Graphic design and typesetting: Full Moon Media

Author's Note

Unless stated otherwise, all Gregg Allman quotes are taken from his 2012 memoir *My Cross To Bear*. Unless stated otherwise, all Butch Trucks, Dickey Betts, Chuck Leavell, Warren Haynes, Jaimoe, Jack Pearson, Marc Quiñones, Derek Trucks and Oteil Burbridge quotes are taken from interviews published in *Hittin' The Note* between 1997 and 2013. All Galadrielle Allman quotes are taken from *Please Be With Me: A Song For My Father Duane Allman* (2014). All chart placings are from *Billboard*.

Also by Andrew Wild

Local History
108 Steps Around Macclesfield (Sigma Press, 1994/2nd edition, Rumble Strips, 2018)
Exploring Chester (Sigma Press, 1996/republication, Rumble Strips, 2018)
Ever Forward (MADS, 1997)

Biographies
Play On (Twelfth Night, 2009)
One for the Record (Avalon, 2013/2nd edition, 2018)
Books About Music
Pink Floyd Song by Song (Fonthill, 2017)
Queen On Track (Sonicbond, 2018)
The Beatles: An A-Z Guide to Every Song (Sonicbond, 2019)
Solo Beatles 1969-1980 On Track (Sonicbond, 2020)
Crosby, Stills and Nash On Track (Sonicbond, 2020)
Dire Straits On Track (Sonicbond, 2021)
Fleetwood Mac in the 1970s (Sonicbond, 2021)
Eric Clapton Solo On Track (Sonicbond, 2021)
Eric Clapton Sessions On Track (Sonicbond, 2022)
Phil Collins In The 1980s (Sonicbond, 2022)
Books About Films
James Bond On Screen (Sonicbond, 2021)
Books About Comics
The Perfect Marvel Comics Collection vol. 1 – 1939-1965 (Rumble Strips, 2022)
The Perfect Marvel Comics Collection vol. 2 – 1966-1973 (Rumble Strips, 2022)
The Perfect Marvel Comics Collection vol. 3 – 1974-1985 (Rumble Strips, 2022)
Plays
The Difficult Crossing (Stagescripts, 2016)
A Difficult Man (Rumble Strips, 2021)

Dedicated to all the brothers we have lost.
And to Amanda, Rosie and Amy, with love.

Acknowledgements

Many grateful thanks to Richard Brent – Executive Director of The Allman Brothers Band Museum at the Big House – and to John Lynskey, former publisher/editor of *Hittin' the Note* magazine, and historian/archivist at the Big House: 2321 Vineville Avenue, Macon, GA, 31204.

Thank you also to Hans van Ryswyk for the peerless DuaneAllman.info website, and for attention to detail in our email exchanges. Gracias to Eric Senich for the Alan Walden book. Greetings Mike Bowen. Hello and thank you to John Ryan the Chicago Kid, for correspondence. Big, big thanks to Art Dobie and Gary Nagle. Kudos to Emma Spires, Gareth Cole, Lee Abraham, Tim Sparks and Mark Spencer for contribution to a lively debate about Duane Allman's slide guitar-playing. Thumbs up to Bob Beatty. Buy his book!

There is a voice from the tomb sweeter than song. There is a remembrance of the dead to which we turn even from the charms of the living.
Washington Irving, *The Sketchbook of Geoffrey Crayon*, 1820

There's wildness, and then there's pandemonium.
Gregory Allman, 2013

Foreword

The Allman Brothers Band was a group like no other. These masters of improvisation defined how rock music should be played in a concert setting for more than four decades.

Founded and led by visionary guitarist Duane Allman in 1969, the band quickly exceeded even *his* lofty expectations. Aided and abetted by his younger brother Gregg on vocals and keyboards, the dual drumming of Butch Trucks and Jaimoe, the rock-bottom bass of Berry Oakley and the lead guitar partnership of Dickey Betts, the sum of the group's talent, far exceeded its considerable individual parts. The ABB blended elements of rock, jazz, blues and country into a volatile musical mixture that left audiences literally worn out. No band played more often, in more places, for anyone who would listen, than the original Allman Brothers did. Their reputation was cemented in July 1971 with the release of *At Fillmore East:* widely considered to be the greatest live performance recording in the history of rock music.

Even after the devastating losses of Duane Allman in October 1971 and Berry Oakley 13 months later, the band found a way to soldier on. Despite these crushing blows, the ABB's level of musicianship remained *non-pareil*. Chuck Leavell, Lamar Williams, Warren Haynes, Allen Woody, Marc Quinones, Oteil Burbridge, Jack Pearson, Derek Trucks and Jimmy Herring maintained the incredible standards set by Duane Allman. The Allman Brothers Band is the only group to place four members in *Rolling Stone*'s list of 100 Greatest Guitarists; what more needs to be said?

In 2014, the ABB called it a career after 45 years, but their legacy lives on. Part of that legacy is the story of the true brotherhood that existed between the band members, the road crew and extended family and friends – and that spirit can be experienced firsthand at the Allman Brothers Band Museum at the Big House. Located at 2321 Vineville Avenue in Macon, Georgia, the Big House served as the centre of the group's universe from 1970 to 1973. It was the ultimate hippie communal living experience – one practised by many bands, including Grateful Dead, Jefferson Airplane, Lynyrd Skynyrd and The Doobie Brothers – but the Big House is the only official rock-&-roll band house museum in the country. Fans come from all over the world to soak up the vibe of the OG Six in the Ramblin' Tudor-style mansion they once called home. Triumph and tragedy, joy and sorrow, loss and rebirth – it all happened at the Big House, and we are proud to carry on that indomitable spirit 50 years later.

Yes, The Allman Brothers Band was a band like no other; and this, a book like no other. Andrew Wild has produced a work worthy of the ABB's Hall-of-Fame status. His focus on detail and facts is astonishing. What Andrew has chronicled for the likes of The Beatles, Eric Clapton, Pink Floyd, Queen and Fleetwood Mac, has been done again in spades with *The Allman Brothers Band On Track*.

It's an honour to write the preface to this book, from Duane Allman's bedroom at the Big House. Savour it, and enjoy every page.

Eat a Peach.

John Lynskey

Former publisher/editor of *Hittin' the Note* magazine, and historian/archivist at the Big House

on track ...
The Allman Brothers Band

Contents

Introduction

In 1973, The Allman Brothers Band were one of the most popular in America. They headlined the Watkins Glen Summer Jam – attended by an estimated 600,000 people – on 28 July, and their album *Brothers and Sisters* was number 1 for five weeks on the *Billboard* listings that summer. The single 'Ramblin' Man' hit 2 in October. The group made the cover of *Newsweek. Rolling Stone* named them 'Band of the Year'.

Their story can only be described as unpredictable. Always a strong live draw since forming in 1969, in the two years prior to Watkins Glen, they had released one of the greatest live albums of all time and lost two founding members in near-identical motorcycle accidents: including guitar genius: 24-year-old Duane Allman. Increased drug use and a ruinous 1976 court case forced the band apart. A three-album reunion between 1978 and 1982, rekindled some of the old fire, but it was their 20th anniversary and second reformation in 1989 that provided a degree of stability and renewed acclaim. The album *Seven Turns* (1990) introduced guitarist/vocalist Warren Haynes to the Allman Brothers Band. Haynes – and later the mercurial Derek Trucks – added a powerful presence after founding-member Dickey Betts was fired in 2000 due to 'creative differences'.

The band's annual residency at the Beacon Theatre in New York City (from 1989) comprised over 200 shows across 25 years. This remarkable series of concerts concluded with the final performance of their career – 28 October 2014, stretching over four hours into the early morning of the 43rd anniversary of Duane Allman's death.

The passing of founder members Butch Trucks and Gregg Allman in 2017 definitively ended the band's story. Their legacy of 11 studio albums, six contemporaneous live albums and several box sets, includes classics such as their self-titled debut, the sophomore *Idlewild South* (their artistic and commercial breakthrough), the definitive live document *At Fillmore East,* and the astounding final album *Hittin' The Note* from 2003.

The Allman Brothers Band was one of the great American rock groups – phenomenal musicians capable of delivering honesty and dynamism, both in performance and on record. As Gregg Allman said, 'If your music doesn't have dynamics, you might as well get another job. Just like the rising and falling of a poem, the music also travels, and you have to feel it'. Their music is the pure distillation of the four main ingredients of American music: blues, rock, jazz and country.

Bob Beatty wrote in *Play All Night!*: 'At times, the guitars stand out. At other times, it's the drums. Sometimes it's Gregg's vocals or the magnificent swirling sound of his Hammond B3. Undergirding it all is a rock-solid foundation of ensemble-playing; each musician making up his part as he goes along. It is a musical conversation, and The Allman Brothers Band are among the premier musical conversationalists in the history of rock music'.

At their best, The Allman Brothers Band transcended genre: they just were.

Before The Allman Brothers Band

Gregg Allman (born 8 December 1947) and his older brother Duane (20 November 1946) were both born in Nashville. In 1949, they moved to Virginia, where their father Willis was killed in a robbery that December. The family returned to Nashville, and from 1955 – with their mother Geraldine studying to qualify as an accountant – the brothers were sent to be educated at Castle Heights Military Academy in Lebanon, Tennessee: 30 miles east of 'Music City'. 'Having my older brother with me was the only thing that saved me', Gregg wrote in his memoir.

The family moved to 100 Van Avenue, Daytona Beach, Florida in 1959. Geraldine lived there until her death in 2015.

Gregg told *Rolling Stone* in 1979:

I didn't start playing music till we moved to Daytona Beach. I started on guitar in the summer of 1960, and Duane picked it up by the fall. I taught him the basics, and he really took a yen to it, quit school… that's all he ever did … many nights I'd wake up and there he'd be, just pickin' away. We listened to Elmore James, Sonny Boy Williamson, Howlin' Wolf, Ray Charles, B.B. King. I guess Little Milton was about my favourite. We went, let's just say, across the tracks. Our mother called it somethin' else. We had to ease over there. and for about 97 cents, you could buy these old albums. I've still got a few of 'em.

Originally, Duane would borrow Gregg's Silvertone guitar, for which he saved hard, and bought from the local Sears store, as Gregg recalled: 'He looks at my guitar and says, 'Now what you got there, baby brother?'. I go, 'Now all right, Duane, that's mine'. He would slip into my room and play it. I swear to God, we had more fights over that guitar than you'd believe'.

Soon, Duane had a guitar of his own. He told *Crawdaddy*:

The guitar saved me from so much grief. I was a hoodlum … then that old guitar came along and I had something to do. When I get pissed off, I just sit down and beat the fire out of some old Jimmy Reed shit instead of going out and drinking and fighting and falling down and going crazy. It would take me all the way, man, and put me on a good note.

'Then not only was there peace in the family', Gregg wrote, 'but we started playing together. I had shown him how to play at the beginning, then he started showing me some licks, and we would just help each other out – that's how we learned'.

Gregg subsequently developed a powerful, distinctive and very soulful singing voice. Their ambitions were heightened during a summer trip back to Nashville to visit their grandparents, as Gregg recalled:

One night, my mother dropped me and my brother off at the Nashville Municipal Auditorium, and we spent a buck and a quarter to sit in the cheap seats. Jackie Wilson was the headliner. Cheap seats or no cheap seats, it was amazing. Next to Jackie was Otis Redding, and Otis just took it, man. He got the whole place singing, and moving faster and faster. My brother was just mesmerized – he was frozen, and he looked stuffed, like a taxidermist had gotten through with him. Nothing on his body moved during the whole concert. That music was in his heart, and it was in mine too. Then we got to playing it, and we realized how important it really was.

They quickly upgraded to electric guitars, courtesy of their doting mother. Gregg was given a Fender Musicmaster, and Duane a cherry-red 1959 Gibson Les Paul Junior. Between them, they played in several short-term bands in Daytona in 1961/1962, including The Kings, The Uniques and The Shufflers – performing wherever they could, including at Y-Teen events at the local YMCA. Duane's school band The Misfits formed back at Castle Heights Military Academy in late-summer 1961. Bass player Mike Johnstone told author Randy Poe: 'We rehearsed down at the auditorium there at the school, and played school dances. We did what I call black rock & roll – the early R&B things: Bobby 'Blue' Bland and Ray Charles and James Brown. I remember we played 'Stormy Monday'. I was coming out of surf music – that was my deal. I got started listening to Chet Atkins, which led me to The Ventures. Duane was into that too, but he was more into B.B. King'.

The Misfits were to add Gregg the following year and perform gigs locally ... until Duane was expelled from school in late 1963. Gregg was also asked to leave soon after, and they returned to Daytona Beach.

No longer in school, Duane and Gregg formed their first serious professional band, The Escorts. The instrumental lineup followed that of the newly-famous Beatles – two guitars, with bass (local musician Van Harrison) and drums (Maynard Portwood). An early recording session – intended as a showcase for prospective live bookings – included covers of The Beatles, Gerry and the Pacemakers, The Searchers and The Righteous Brothers. They also performed songs by Roy Orbison, The Impressions, The Yardbirds, The Troggs and others. Gregg Allman:

We did a whole bunch of old R&B love songs – stuff like 'Pretty Woman', 'I've Been Trying', 'Hi-Heel Sneakers' and 'You've Lost That Lovin' Feeling', which we butchered. 'Are You Sincere', by Lenny Welch, was one of my brother's choices, and we did 'This Boy' by The Beatles because we had to play enough Beatles songs. We did some instrumentals as well, including 'Memphis' and our version of the theme from *Goldfinger*. We'd also do 'Wild Thing', which got us real close to getting fired several times. Most clubs just wanted us to be a jukebox onstage, and we were a great one.

The Escorts' biggest break was in spring 1965 when they opened for The Beach Boys in Daytona Beach. This band was renamed The Allman Joys in summer 1965, now with Bob Keller on bass. A new demo tape signalled a move away from the British Invasion towards the American music of The Nashville Teens, Buck Owens, Lonnie Mack, Sir Douglas Quintet and Bobby 'Blue' Bland. Gregg wrote in his memoir: 'We were doing 'Turn On Your Love Light', because we had heard Bobby 'Blue' Bland do it. And man, you talk about an original talent – there will be – and can be – only one Bobby 'Blue' Bland'.

In writer/director Cameron Crowe's 1989 book *The Day The Music Died*, Tom Petty (in 1965 an underage upstart living in Jacksonville) remembers hoisting himself up on a cement wall to see a frat dance where the Allman Joys appeared: 'Duane just stood there, off to the side, ripping through these great leads, and there was his baby-faced little brother, who opened his mouth and sounded like Joe Tex'.

The Allmans moved to Los Angeles in mid-1966, with Portwood and Keller replaced by Bill Connell and Mike Alexander. They later recorded in Nashville at a studio called Bradley's Barn: including an incendiary version of Willie Dixon's 'Spoonful', which was released as a single. Several other tracks surfaced years later on the album *Early Allman*. Six can be heard on the 2013 retrospective *Skydog*. 'We made it clear that we never wanted those released', Gregg said. 'They were terrible songs, just awful'.

Around this time or possibly earlier, Gregg and Duane first met future Allman Brothers Band drummer Claude Hudson 'Butch' Trucks, when Trucks' band the Bitter Ind (for 'individual') crossed paths with The Allman Joys on the Florida club circuit. As Gregg later wrote, 'Musicians find musicians, and I met every one of them in Daytona – black, white, and everything in between'. Butch Trucks told *Rolling Stone* in June 2009:

(Duane) was this incredibly charismatic, almost messianic type of personality. He was more than a bandleader, he was a guy who could really change you. There are very, very few people you meet like that in your lifetime. If I hadn't met him, I'd be teaching school, I don't doubt that. I can still remember the day he reached in and flicked a switch in me that changed me from being a really nervous introverted drummer, to playing with confidence. Most people don't really have it in them to let it all hang out. That's why most people aren't professional musicians. They asked Mark Twain what it took to be successful, and he said, 'That's easy: all you have to be is ignorant and cocky'. You have to not be afraid, and at the time, I was very afraid. So we were jamming one day, and it wasn't going anywhere, and Duane turned around and stared me in the eye and played this lick. It was like a challenge, like, 'Come on, motherfucker!'. I backed off, and he did it again, and again, and after a while I got mad and I started hitting the drums like I was slapping him on the side of the head. And I forgot about the nervousness and that I was afraid, and the jam got going, and he pointed a finger at me and said, 'There you go'. And a light bulb went off. I made a decision then: 'I can play'.

Trucks' bandmates were bassist David Brown and guitarist Scott Boyer. All three attended high school and Florida State University together. Boyer told Randy Poe: 'I'd been playing coffee houses and stuff like that. I knew all these Bob Dylan songs. It was around then that The Byrds came in, and The Lovin' Spoonful. So David approached me with the idea of the three of us getting together and me gettin' an electric guitar, and they'd back me up on bass and drums, and we'd make some money off this folk-rock thing. That was pretty much how it all got started'.

They were hired for a concert at the Martinique: Daytona's biggest club. Trucks told Poe: 'We decided to go to Daytona and hit it big. We started playing our set, and in comes... some presence. You'da thought The Beatles just came in. I mean, it was like the Red Sea parting – people letting them come in and sit down. It was very obvious that there were some personages in the audience. It turned out to be The Allman Joys – Duane and Gregg Allman'. Butch made friends with the brothers, and sat in with The Allman Joys at least once. For now, their paths diverged.

The Allman Joys ultimately evolved into Hour Glass when Gregg and Duane hooked up with a band called The Men-Its in St. Louis. Gregg moved to organ, and the balance of the band was made up of Duane, keyboardist Paul Hornsby, bass player Mabron McKinney (later switched for Pete Carr) and drummer Johnny Sandlin. This new band went through a number of names (The Five Men-Its, The Almanac, even The Allman Joys for a while) before settling on Hour Glass when they secured a record deal with Liberty Records in Los Angeles in mid-1967. They made their Los Angeles concert debut supporting The Doors at the Hullabaloo Club on Sunset Boulevard: probably on 8 June.

The band recorded two albums for Liberty. *Hour Glass* (recorded August 1967; released October 1967) mostly contains covers of soul songs by writers such as Curtis Mayfield, Jimmy Radcliffe and Goffin/King. It fails to realise the band's potential, despite Gregg Allman's impressive vocals. As Randy Poe wrote, it's 'an album consisting of a hodgepodge of genres performed by a band being pulled in various musical directions by a producer with no apparent focus'. The much more mature *Power Of Love* (recorded January 1968; released March 1968) features liner notes by Neil Young and seven original songs by Gregg Allman, who later described the two Hour Glass albums as 'a shit sandwich'.

Duane meanwhile – always a music fan as much as a professional – attended a concert by blues musician Taj Mahal, where Duane experienced an epiphany. Mahal sang his arrangement of Blind Willie McTell's 'Statesboro Blues', complete with slide guitar by band member Jesse Ed Davis. Paul Hornsby recalls: 'He made quite an impression on Duane. From the first time that we saw them, we picked up 'Statesboro Blues'. Taj was doing that, and from then on, we claimed that song. That was the first song that Duane played slide on in Hour Glass. Of course, now when you think of 'Statesboro Blues' you think of the Allman Brothers version, but Taj was doing it before them. We pretty much did the same arrangement as Taj'.

As the story goes, Duane taught himself to play slide guitar on his 21st birthday – 20 November 1967 – when he was recovering from an elbow injury. Gregg brought him the self-titled debut album by Taj Mahal and a bottle of Coricidin pills. Duane emptied and washed the pill bottle, and used it as a slide, to play along with Mahal's slick version of Blind Willie McTell's 'Statesboro Blues'. It's a tall tale, as *Taj Mahal* was not released until early-1968. Bill McEuan – manager of The Nitty Gritty Dirt Band – knew the Allmans in this period, and claims that Duane 'got the idea for 'Statesboro Blues' after listening to the Folkways album *The Country Blues*. This might be true, but the Taj Mahal version is a clear and obvious inspiration on the Allmans' later arrangement. Duane himself said in a radio interview with Ellen Mandel in 1970:

I heard Ry Cooder playing some time ago, and I said, 'Man that's for me'. And I got me a bottle and went in the house for about three weeks, and I said, 'Hey man, we've got to learn the songs – the blues to play on the stage. I love this. This is a gas'. So we started doing it, and for a while, it was everybody looking at me and thinking, 'Oh no! He's getting ready to do it again!'. Everybody just lowered their heads – start it off fast and get it over with. But then I got a little better at it and improved it, but now everybody's blowing it all out of proportion. It's just fine for me as a relief from the other kind of playing.

Cooder played with Taj Mahal in the Los Angeles-based band The Rising Sons in 1965/1966, but he didn't play much slide at that time. Allman saw Taj Mahal's band – with Jesse Ed Davis – in Los Angeles, and may well be confusing Davis with Cooder. Paul Hornsby says Duane first wanted to play slide after hearing 'Beck's Bolero' on *Truth* by The Jeff Beck Group. This was released in July 1968, by which time Hour Glass had split up. The real story is perhaps an amalgamation of all of these threads.

Hour Glass opened for some of the biggest acts of the day – Big Brother and the Holding Company, Jefferson Airplane, The Animals and Buffalo Springfield. A series of self-funded demos recorded at FAME (Florence Alabama Music Enterprises) Studios in Muscle Shoals, Alabama in April 1968, remained unreleased, although a scintillating medley of three B.B. King songs became a highlight of *Duane Allman: An Anthology*, released in 1972. This is perhaps the only Hour Glass studio cut that suggests their power as a live band. Other songs from these 1968 sessions have been included on *An Anthology Volume II* and the *Dreams* box set.

But Liberty Records never really understood the band's objectives, and they disbanded in mid-1968. Gregg subsequently returned to Los Angeles to record a solo album to fulfil his obligation to Liberty. These songs – including, remarkably, a version of Tammy Wynette's 'D-I-V-O-R-C-E' – are an indication of just how little Liberty understood Gregg Allman. 11 tracks from these sessions were released as part of the 1992 reissue of the Hour Glass back catalogue.

Duane returned to Florida and hooked up with drummer and old friend Butch Trucks. Allman agreed to work on demos with Trucks' band: now renamed 31st of February. Gregg also joined these sessions. They recorded nine songs in September 1968: eventually released in 1972 on the album *Duane & Gregg Allman*. Notable tracks include a powerful version of Tim Rose' folk-rock standard 'Morning Dew', the soulful slow blues 'Nobody Knows You When You're Down and Out' (which Duane later recorded with Derek and the Dominoes in a very similar arrangement), and an early version of 'Melissa' which even then sounded like a stone-cold classic and included Duane's first recorded slide guitar-playing.

With Gregg back in California completing his solo commitments, Duane received a phone call from FAME Studios owner Rick Hall, who'd been impressed by Duane's playing on the B.B. King medley and wondered if Duane wanted a job as a session player. Over the next two years, Duane Allman added his unmistakable guitar-playing to songs on many sessions. The first to be released was 'The Road of Love' by Clarence Carter: recorded 12 November 1968. Galadrielle Allman:

Duane loved Clarence Carter, and when he heard he was coming in, he turned up the heat and Rick told him he could play on the session. They cut a real blues thing called 'Road Of Love', and Duane's playing really shined. Rick was very impressed. In the middle of the song, Carter even sang out, 'I like what I'm listening to right now' after Duane's slide solo: a blast of passion in the middle of a simple funky groove. Duane brought that track to life.

Duane's superlative performance on Wilson Pickett's 'Hey Jude', dates from either 17 or 27 November 1968 (sources differ). Galadrielle writes: 'On 'Hey Jude', Duane sounds like he's being released – clearly excited by the energy radiating from Wilson Pickett. Duane sat on a small amp facing him, and they locked in, matching each other's intensity and driving each other to a fever pitch. That feeling of expanding the possibility of a song with his playing, pointed the way forward for Duane. His fierce solo at the end of the cut was the true beginning of his career. Everyone who heard it, wanted to know who he was. It opened doors for him'.

Sessions with Arthur Conley, Aretha Franklin, King Curtis and many others, quickly followed. Boz Scaggs' astounding 'Loan Me A Dime' dates from May 1969. Many of these are collected on the tremendous 1972 compilation *Duane Allman – An Anthology*. Fans with deeper pockets should seek out the 7-CD box set *Skydog* (2013), which includes a wide selection of Allman's session work along with tracks by The Escorts, The Allman Joys, Hour Glass and 31st of February.

Despite the income, stability and reputation that these sessions brought, Duane missed playing live with his own band. FAME signed Duane to a five-year recording contract in December 1968, with the view that he would form and lead a band of his own. Early in the new year, Allman recruited drummer

Jai Johanny 'Jaimoe' Johanson, at the suggestion of local booking agent and studio owner Phil Walden. Jaimoe had toured with Otis Redding, Percy Sledge, Clarence Carter and Joe Tex, and had been employed by Walden as a session drummer following a recommendation from Sledge's tour manager Twiggs Lyndon. In 2017, Jaimoe told *Mississippi Today* that between sessions, Duane would roll that Fender Twin amplifier 'out of the studio over to where I was, and I found out what jazz is. Music that comes out of this country is music that makes you happy, sad and the rest of it. Jazz is American music – hillbilly, hip hop, rhythm and blues: it's all jazz. And I learned it in search of jazz'.

Duane next called up Berry Oakley. Oakley was a bass guitarist with an acute sense of melody. He'd previously been lead guitarist in several bands in his native Chicago, and played bass with the same drive and attack. Oakley met Duane and Gregg Allman in July 1968 at the Comic Book Club in Jacksonville when he was playing with a band called Second Coming. Despite his youth, Oakley was a seasoned professional, joining Tommy Roe's band in 1965, aged 17. Jaimoe recalled: 'It had been so great playing with Duane, but I thought we'd never find a bass player who could do the stuff that we were doing. When Berry arrived (in January 1969), it was amazing. It was like, 'Where did this dude come from?'. It became a whole different ball game, and at that point, my perspective changed'.

In February 1969, Duane recorded eight songs using Oakley and two former members of Hour Glass: Johnny Sandlin and Paul Hornsby. A cover of St. Louis Jimmy Oden's 'Goin' Down Slow' can be heard on 1972's *Duane Allman: An Anthology*, and his own composition 'Happily Married Man' and a version of Chuck Berry's 'No Money Down' are included on *An Anthology Volume II* (1974). These three tracks can also be heard on the *Sky Dog* box set. Another song – 'Steal Away' – was planned for the *Dreams* box set, but remains unreleased. It can be found online if you know where to look.

In this period, Duane frequently returned to Jacksonville to hang out with Butch Trucks, and jam with Oakley and his Second Coming bandmates, including guitarist Dickey Betts and pianist Reese Wynans. Betts said: For a period of about two years, Duane would just show up and sit in. Duane has that real clear sound, although it had more of a blues edge to it, and my style had that country kind of thing. But they worked together'.

In early-March 1969, Duane took Jaimoe to Florida. Butch said: 'One day there's a knock at my door, and it's Duane. He's got this big black guy with him with this tank top on him, you know, and he looked like Schwarzenegger or something – really muscle-bound – and he's got these bear claws around his neck and everything. And Duane says, 'Hey Jaimoe, this is my old drummer Butch. Butch, this is my new drummer Jaimoe'. With my old Southern Baptist sensitivities, I figure I got this militant African guy here who's gonna rip my head off. He was mean-lookin!'. He wound up staying for two weeks – he didn't leave! But once he opened up and started talking, I mean, we just hit it right off '.

Then on 23 March 1969, Duane Allman called on Butch Trucks and Jaimoe for a private rehearsal session at Butch's residence, the Gray House at 2844

Riverside Avenue, Jacksonville. Oakley, Betts and Wynans also took part. Duane later spoke about this session: 'We set up the equipment and whipped into a little jam, and it lasted two and a half hours. When we finally quit, nobody said a word, man. Everybody was speechless. Nobody'd ever done anything like that before. It really frightened the shit out of everybody'.

Butch recalled in 1979: 'We were all in this room afterward, and Duane got in the doorway and said, 'Anybody in this room that's not gonna play in my band, you're gonna have to fight your way out'. And that was it. It was like being born again at a revival meeting; we got saved that day'.

'Right then, I knew', Duane recalled later. 'I said, 'Man, here it is, here it is!'. The only thing is, we need a singer'.

That singer – 'baby brother' Gregg Allman – was recalled from Los Angeles. Duane called him up. Gregg wrote in a letter to Cameron Crowe in 1973: 'I had been building the nerve to put a pistol to my head. Then Duane called and told me he had a band. I put my thumb out and caught the first thing smokin' for Jacksonville'. Gregg flew (or hitched or drove or blagged a ride) back to Florida to meet up with Duane's new band on 26 March 1969.

Galadrielle Allman:

In anticipation of Gregg's arrival, they dusted off an old country-blues tune that Muddy Waters had electrified first – common ground for them to stand on together – a song called 'Trouble No More'. Duane handed Gregg the lyrics he had written out by hand.

Gregg:

I was absolutely elated when I walked into that room and saw the whole band there. Of course, when you walk into a room and everybody knows everybody else except you, it's tough, especially when you're as shy as I am. It was real tense. You could have cut it with a knife.

Galadrielle:

There was no way out, so Gregg sang. He poured his anger and stress into the song, and it fuelled him. He dug into the deepest, most guttural and bluesy side of his voice, and unleashed everything he had. The smile that spread across Duane's face, flashed all the way across the room. Duane was so thrilled when he was done he grabbed Gregg's face in both hands, and kissed him on the lips.

Gregg:

They counted off, and I did my damnedest. I'd never heard or sung this song before, but by God I did it. I shut my eyes and sang, and at the end of that, there was just a long silence. At that moment, we knew what we had.

Gregg's arrival pulled the band together, but Reese Wynans was deemed surplus to requirements. He joined Boz Scaggs' band, and later worked, toured and recorded with Stevie Ray Vaughan (1985-1990) and Joe Bonamassa (since 2015).

The Allman Brothers Band's first lineup was therefore established as Duane Allman (22), Gregg Allman (21), Dickey Betts (25), Jaimoe (24), Berry Oakley (20) and Butch Trucks (21). Though the band was an equal six-way partnership, Duane was the leader.

Author Bob Beatty wrote:

In founding the Allman Brothers Band, Duane carved a niche that allowed pursuit of his musical vision – one based on his band members' abilities and an original take on their combined musical roots. Duane chose bandmates who pushed musical boundaries and drew inspiration from the guitar-based free-form attacks of British blues groups like, notably, Cream. To this mix he added an important new element: dual lead guitars. In Dickey Betts, Duane brought in a player he and everyone else acknowledged as his equal. Bassist Berry Oakley – himself a former lead guitarist – commanded the bass as a third lead instrument; gave the band three guitar soloists. Two drummers – a rare combination in rock – provided a foundation that simultaneously grounded the band rhythmically, as it propelled the music forward with an unusually powerful sound. Although he was its star, Duane built The Allman Brothers Band as a band of musical equals.

Trucks said: '[Duane] really had a lot of problems with the name The Allman Brothers Band. He didn't want to call it that. He really wanted to find a name for the band that didn't call attention to himself, and we couldn't come up with anything'.

Thankfully the suggestions Almanac and Beelzebub were rejected.

In 2017, Trucks explained to *American Blues Scene* how the band's different influences worked together:

We kinda picked up where Cream left off. Cream opened the door to improvisation in rock and roll. But, it was strictly blues. So, when they jammed, they pretty much just jammed on one chord. It was pretty mono-dynamic too. It was brand new, though; nobody had ever taken an old blues song, an old Robert Johnson song, and then stretched it for 15 minutes, you know? But they did. Duane had kinda cut his eye teeth on The Yardbirds, so Clapton, Jeff Beck and Jimmy Page were all big influences. Then we started playing and jamming like that. Jaimoe turned us on to Charlie Parker, John Coltrane, Miles Davis, Cannonball (Adderley), Herbie Hancock, Corea and people like this. Our eyes popped open and we went, 'Damn!', we can do that. We can take what Cream did and add dynamics to it, starting the solo way down, very quiet, and build and build it. Then Duane and Dickey – one of them would play something, and the other one pick up on it and they'd jump right on it. It was kind of the thing that 'Trane and Cannonball would do when they would jam together. So, adding jazz to the mix of blues, rock and roll, rhythm and blues, a little country, and then mixing them all together. But it was that jazz element that I think made The Allman Brothers something brand new that no one had ever heard before.

Many years later, Duane's daughter Galadrielle eloquently wrote:

Duane played guitar so beautifully, the world came to him. His remarkable talent brought him the opportunity to build a band of his own, and he formed a group of players that matched his skill and his commitment to playing, note for note. They raised the bar for one another, each honing his skill against the other, blade against stone. The powerful chemistry between the Brothers came together so fast it seemed magical and destined. Dickey's strengths and style were different than Duane's. Dickey had a kind of fight in him that set off Duane's fluidity in a remarkable way. Dickey's tone and attack drew from a country root, while Duane was digging deeply into the blues. The conversation between their sounds was dynamic and fascinating, and the music that unfolded during their Jacksonville jams began to shift the direction Duane thought his band would take.

Berry Oakley is quoted in Alan Paul's *One Way Out*: 'Each man in the group has been a musician for years, working in bar bands, country and jazz groups, the whole route. Our music just sort of evolved out of that mixture. It was a sound that was truly unique to the band'.

Gregg brought 'Dreams' and 'No Cross To Bear' (written in California), and composed 'Whipping Post' in the days after joining the band. Within a week, they'd performed their first gig: as guests for Second Coming.

FAME Records owner Rick Hall had anticipated Duane Allman founding a power trio. He listened to Allman's solo recordings and decided to cut his losses. He offered Allman's contract to Jerry Wexler at Atlantic Records. Wexler had been impressed with 'Hey Jude', and had met Duane at an Aretha Franklin session in New York. Duane told John Tiven at the *New Haven Rock Press* in December 1970 that getting with Atlantic Records was the big break: 'Atlantic, man, they dig our music. And Ahmet, the President, he loves to listen to good sides, man. You go right to him and bang on his door. 'Ahmet, Ahmet, something's screwed', and he says, 'What?'. You say, 'This', and he says, 'We'll change it', and it's done; you don't have to fool around. There ain't none of that crap. He's solid and it's a good label'.

Atlantic funded Phil Walden's newly-formed Capricorn Records as a local base for the Allman Brothers Band, and offered studio time and distribution. Ahmet Ertegun told *Hittin' The Note* in 2005: 'We were completely supportive of the idea of Phil and (business partner) Frank (Fenter) creating a label that we would be involved in. I felt that it would have a very powerful and strong

presence because... they had The Allman Brothers. I think that Capricorn Records created an important part of rock and roll history'.

Capricorn were based in Macon, Georgia: 80 miles southwest of Atlanta. The entire Allman Brothers Band promptly moved to the town, into Twiggs Lyndon's two-room apartment at 309 College Street. Dickey Betts recalled: 'When first moved to Macon, we all lived in this little apartment with mattresses on the floor, a radio and a coke machine. We lived together and we played music. That's all we did'.

The band's first recordings date from late-April – demos of 'Don't Want You No More', 'It's Not My Cross To Bear', 'Trouble No More' and 'Dreams'.

Bob Beatty:

The tracks present a band in the earliest stages of its development, and it is hardly surprising that the sound is somewhat tentative at times. The group had been together for less than a month, and only Duane, Gregg and Butch had any appreciable studio experience. Of the four songs, only 'Dreams' emerged markedly different on the band's debut album, with Dickey forgoing the wah-wah pedal and Duane adding a slide solo. Duane played slide with swagger on 'Trouble No More'. An instrumental – 'Don't Want You No More' – clocked in at a tight two minutes. Gregg's 'It's Not My Cross To Bear' sounds more contemplative than the bolder version they recorded later in the year.

Butch Trucks recalled in 2009: 'We knew the band was fucking good. We'd all been in different bands trying to be stars, and they all sucked. This was finally a band where we really enjoyed playing. The record company took one look at Gregg and said, 'Get that guy out from behind the organ, and stick a salami down his pants'. But we said, 'Screw it'. It was about the music'.

Part I: 26 March 1969 – 4 May 1976

The Allman Brothers Band (1969)

Personnel:
Duane Allman: lead and slide guitar
Gregg Allman: organ, piano, vocals
Dickey Betts: lead guitar
Jaimoe: drums, congas, timbales
Berry Oakley: bass
Butch Trucks: drums
Recorded August 1969 at Atlantic Studios, New York City
Producer: Adrian Barber
Release date: November 1969
Chart position: 188

> The Allman Brothers are a rather heavy white blues group out of Muscle
> Shoals. They look like the post-teen punk band rehearsing next door, and
> there is little in their music that we haven't heard before. And both they and
> their album are a gas.
> **Lester Bangs, *Rolling Stone*, 21 February 1970**

The Allman Brothers Band was not recorded in Nashville, Daytona Beach,
Macon or Muscle Shoals, but in New York City over two weeks in summer
1969. The reason for the move north was, principally, to work with Tom
Dowd. One of the most important producers of the post-war era, Dowd had
been active at Atlantic for 20 years at this point, and engineered or produced
recordings for artists as diverse as Ray Charles, The Drifters, The Coasters, Ruth
Brown, Bobby Darin, John Coltrane, Ornette Coleman, Thelonious Monk,
Charlie Parker and Cream. But Dowd was called away at the last moment. He
told *Hittin' The Note* in 1994:

> I was supposed to have done the first album with the band up in New York,
> but some way or other I got detoured. Jerry Wexler made a deal to keep them
> in the studio for three or four days when they were supposed to be with me.
> But I had a panic call, and I couldn't tell you to this day whether it was Muscle
> Shoals or Memphis, but all of a sudden, 'Hey Dowd, get your ass down there.
> They need you'. So the chap who was working with me – Adrian Barber – and
> his crew did the first Allman Brothers album in three days in the New York
> studio.

Barber had an impressive pedigree as a peer of The Beatles, and member of
The Big Three: one of the most successful Liverpool bands of the early 1960s.
Barber recorded some of the Beatles' Hamburg performances in December

1962, which were eventually issued as *Live! at the Star-Club in Hamburg, Germany; 1962*. By 1968, Barber was employed as a recording engineer and producer for Atlantic Records. He recorded live concerts by Cream, for their final album *Goodbye*.

Sessions for *The Allman Brothers Band* began on Wednesday, 3 August 1969, with an arrangement of the Spencer Davis Group's 'Don't Want You No More' segueing into Gregg's 'It's Not My Cross To Bear'. A version of 'Dreams' was recorded on the same day. 'Black Hearted Woman' and 'Trouble No More' date from 5 August, with the monumental 'Whipping Post' recorded two days later along with an unused take of 'Statesboro Blues'. 'Every Hungry Woman' was laid down on 10 August, and the recording on 12 August 1969 of the familiar classic version of 'Dreams', concluded six days of sessions.

The Allman Brothers Band was released on 4 November 1969 but sold poorly – barely reaching the bottom rungs of the US albums chart.

'Don't Want You No More' (Spencer Davis, Edward Hardin)

The sheer power of The Allman Brothers Band is demonstrated on this bold, powerful instrumental overture to 'It's Not My Cross To Bear'. It opens with a strong riff before dropping to a Latin rhythm with jazz-like organ licks. The song was originally released – with vocals – by the post-Steve Winwood Spencer Davis Group as the B-side of their single 'Time Seller' in July 1967. It was also performed by Betts and Oakley in their pre-ABB band Second Coming – there is a recording claiming to be from 30 March 1969, with Duane, Butch and Jaimoe sitting in with Second Coming, where a nine-minute 'Don't Want You No More' (with vocals) opens the set.

'It's Not My Cross To Bear' (Gregg Allman)

'Don't Want You No More' segues into 'It's Not My Cross To Bear', setting out the band's stall of shuffling rock dynamics, blues guitar and soul-inspired vocals from 22-year-old Gregg Allman. This was one of two songs Gregg brought from Los Angeles to Jacksonville when called to join the band in March 1969. It's dominated by his fatigued singing and Duane's beautiful, lyrical, clean guitar-playing. Dickey Betts also takes a short solo, but his playing is not yet as distinctive or fluid as it would soon become.

Guitar World said in 2017:

No song better encapsulates the way in which The Allman Brothers Band delivered on the elusive goal of countless hippie rockers who loved Muddy Waters: playing blues that were equally original and rooted in the classics.

There are two pre-ABB versions of the song. It was first recorded for Gregg's unreleased solo album for Liberty Records: this very polite version can be heard on the reissue of Hour Glass's *Power Of Love*. Gregg also recorded a rough but powerful demo in Los Angeles just before leaving to join ABB.

This can be heard on the out-of-print 1997 compilation *One More Try: An Anthology*.

'Black Hearted Woman' (Gregg Allman)
Released as a single (edited), March 1970. Did not chart.
Duane and Dickey's Hendrix-inspired harmony guitars drive this tightly arranged up-tempo track which has a very loud, live feel. The supremely tight rhythm section is the rock-solid foundation for the arrangement – Trucks holds down the rhythm, Jaimoe punctuates with percussive flourishes, Oakley's bass sits in the pocket, Duane and Dickey let their fiery guitars fly, and Gregg groans the blues. Perfect.

'Trouble No More' (Muddy Waters)
This was first recorded by blues legend Muddy Waters in 1955. Its composition is based on an older country blues by Sleepy John Estes: the 1935 classic 'Someday Baby Blues'. Here, The Allman Brothers Band display an authentic feel for black music that the much-touted British blues musicians such as John Mayall´s Bluesbreakers, Cream, Fleetwood Mac, Ten Years After and Free tried hard to emulate.

Duane Allman plays slide guitar here, and the arrangement is darker and slower than Waters' perky original. Estes' version, though, is sublime.

An early version from April's demo sessions at Capricorn is included on the *Trouble No More* box set.

'Every Hungry Woman' (Gregg Allman)
Perhaps the album's least impressive track, 'Every Hungry Woman' looks back to the musical milieu of 1967/1968 rather than looking forward with something new. It is mid-tempo blues rock, driven by a catchy riff, and featuring heavily-echoed vocals and tightly-arranged organ and slide guitar. Duane and Dickey trade furious eight-bar solos (2:00 to 2:26) before displaying some astounding harmony playing.

The 1973 mix on *Beginnings* is dryer and more organic.

'Dreams' (Gregg Allman)
'Dreams' is perhaps the most important song on the album: the archetypal Allman Brothers Band track, this is the one to play to newbies. The song was written in Los Angeles during the inconclusive sessions for Gregg's solo album. He later wrote, 'I showed them 'Dreams', and let me tell you, they joined right in. We learned that song the way you hear it today, and I was in, brother'.

The bittersweet verses are based on a simple two-chord organ pattern with an insistent bass pattern *borrowed* from Miles Davis' 'All Blues', with which 'Dreams' also shares a mood and tempo. The arrangement's simplicity allows for extensive jazz-based soloing in waltz time: the perfect jam track. As Duane

23

once said about this song: 'If you can get the music flowing out there where you don't have to listen to it, it just takes you away'.

Just one more mornin', I had to wake up with the blues
Pulled myself outta bed, put on my walkin' shoes
Went up on the mountain to see what I could see
The whole world was fallin' right down in front of me

Gregg wrote in his memoir:

The words to 'Dreams' are completely true. At that time, I was staying up at Julia Brose's place. She was very pretty, and she lived up off of Laurel Canyon. You'd go up there, and on this little hill was a little tiny shack, just big enough for a very romantic hideaway. When I was staying up there, when I woke up and my eyes would open, I would be looking down the mountain. If it was raining, there would be mudslides and all that. That must have been in my mind when I sat down.

The chorus lifts then descends, with powerful dynamics and a strong vocal from Gregg.

'Cause I've a hunger for the dreams, I'll never see
Ah, help me Baby, or this will surely be the end of me

The guitar solo from 1:42 to 4:30 is pure Duane Allman. According to Gregg's memoir, Dickey Betts does not play on 'Dreams':

Back then, there was no lingering tension between any of us, and that included Dickey, who has always been a real hothead: even then. Instead of working things out, he'd work them out with his fists, or screaming, or kicking some ass. The fact is, me and Dickey hardly ever said anything, not while Duane was around, anyway. I can't remember Dickey having any big blowups while Duane was alive. No sooner do we get (into Atlantic studios) than Dickey set his guitar down and said, 'Man, there ain't no windows in this place – it's like a padded cell'. He got his 335 unpacked, took it out, and hit a few licks. Of course, it sounded dead, because there were all these baffles around. I'm not sure what song we started with, but I know 'Dreams' was up toward the front, because Dickey Betts isn't on the recording of 'Dreams'. He finally packed up his guitar, didn't say a thing, and walked out. Duane played all the guitar that you hear on 'Dreams'.

Duane plays a restrained *straight* solo: all string bends and glissandos. He picks up his slide at 3:12 to play one of the great slide guitar solos of all time. Allman proves here that technique is nothing without feel: never once

do you feel that he is showboating. His playing is fully integral to the band's performance – he sits within the song and serves the band, not the opposite. Delicious.

'Whipping Post' (Gregg Allman)
The immortal 'Whipping Post' ends the album with a flourish. It was written in March 1969, just as 21-year-old Gregg Allman joined his brother's band. Originally a slow blues ballad, Berry Oakley asked to take the song away, and overnight reworked the introduction into the odd time signature of 11/8. Butch Trucks told *American Blues Scene in* January 2017:

Gregg almost quit the band the second day that he showed up in Jacksonville, because of what we did to 'Whipping Post'. Obviously, the 'Whipping Post' people *know,* is not a slow ballad. We took that thing and did what we did to it, we went back and Gregg was packing up his suitcase, and Duane said, 'What the hell are you doing?', and he said, 'I'm going back to L.A.. I'm not gonna have you guys ruining my music like that!'. And Duane just told him, 'You sit your sorry ass down. If you are very lucky, you hang around and we're gonna make you a star'.

Gregg recalled:

My brother was staying with this artist chick who lived down the street from Butch, so I had a place to stay too. This was in Arlington, which is a suburb of Jacksonville. I laid me down to go to sleep on my attic couch, and I dozed off for a while. All of a sudden I woke up, because a song had me by the ass. The intro had three sets of three, and two little steps that allowed you to jump back up on the next triad. I thought it was different, and I love different things. It hit me like a ton of bricks. I wish the rest of them had come like this – it was all right there in my head. All I had to do was write it down so I wouldn't forget it by the morning.

That off-kilter 3-3-3-2 groove – built as each instrument enters in turn – the simple chord progression and dynamic arrangement allowed 'Whipping Post' to become a staple of the band's live shows, where 20-minute versions were common.

Again, the song highlights the band's combined strengths – Gregg's passionate vocals, Duane and Dickey's fluid guitar interplay, and the rhythm section's unique mix of syncopation and composure. In particular, Duane's fiery first solo (starting at 1:47) is matched by Dickey's more-measured approach (starting at 3:19). After what sounds like at edit (3:48), the whole band climbs in four-note stages – tightly arranged and brilliantly performed – before Gregg yells one final chorus and the band relax into a gentle conclusion. This is amazing stuff. However you analyse it, 'Whipping Post' is one of the great rock songs of the late-1960s – heavy, powerful, full of soul and drive, dynamic, cathartic, heartbreaking, uplifting. It's a classic in anyone's book.

'Whipping Post' demonstrates why The Allman Brothers transcended the limiting catch-all term Southern rock. It's a rock song that combines substantial elements of the blues, hard rock, jazz fusion, gospel, country and soul music (not to mention Southern gothic fiction) into a combustible testament to rage. The protagonist sounds like he's about to go over the edge: perhaps capable of murder, at having been mistreated by a woman. The musical maelstrom – the unrelenting rhythm section, blistering lead guitars, swirling organ and vocals that are alternately weary and aggressive – seems to mirror the turmoil stirred up in the man:

> I've been run down, I've been lied to
> And I don't know why I let that mean woman make me a fool
> She took all my money, wrecked my new car
> And now she's with one of my good-time buddies
> Drinking in some cross-town bar

Gregg Allman re-recorded the song for his 1997 album *Searching for Simplicity*. This version has a jazz-like groove, but reworks it into 4/4 time instead of the triple time of the original composition.

Idlewild South (1970)

Personnel:
Duane Allman: lead and slide guitar
Gregg Allman: organ, piano, vocals
Dickey Betts: lead guitar
Jaimoe: drums, congas, timbales
Berry Oakley: bass
Butch Trucks: drums
Thom Doucette: harmonica on 'Don't Keep Me Wonderin''
Recorded February- July 1970 at Capricorn Sound, Macon; Criteria, Miami; Atlantic
South, Miami, Florida; Regent Sound, New York
Producer: Tom Dowd; Joel Dorn ('Please Call Home')
Release date: September 1970
Chart position: 38

Idlewild South marks the start of The Allman Brothers' residence at the Big
House at 2321 Vineville Avenue in Macon, Georgia. Berry Oakley's wife Linda
and sister Candace, and Duane's girlfriend Donna Roosman, rented the house,
which was built in 1900. Berry and Duane moved in with their partners and
children. Gregg followed soon after, entering into a relationship with Candace.
The band's road manager, Willie Perkins: 'The Big House really was a big
house, with 19 rooms and 6,000 square feet of space. The house features high
ceilings, intricate woodworking and wainscotting, and colourful stained-glass
windows on theulfilmene landings on all three of its floors'.
    The Big House provided the band's HQ and rehearsal space, and was where
many of the *Idlewild South* songs were conceived and shaped. Gregg recalled:
'It was a big place. I remember thinking that we could put the whole band
in there, but we didn't want to be on top of each other all the time, since we
travelled like that. The Big House – as we came to call it – was a place for all of
us to hang, but it was really Oakley's place'.
    The album title comes from the band's nickname for a rustic cabin they used
for rehearsals. The comings and goings at the cabin reminded them of New
York City's Idlewild airport. Scott Boyer described the cabin, in the 2006 book
Skydog: The Duane Allman Story:

> It was like a hunting cabin. The back of the house had a porch that was built
> out over a man-made lake that was maybe five or six acres. It was a cabin
> made out of old pinewood, and it had been there for a long time ... The
> Allman Brothers used it as a rehearsal facility – that and a place to go maybe
> to consume a little something that wasn't quite legal. There were parties out
> there.

Idlewild South was produced by Tom Dowd, initially at Capricorn Studios in
Macon. Sessions moved to Criteria Studios in Miami in mid-March. 'Please Call

Home' originated in New York City, and was produced by Atlantic's in-house jazz specialist Joel Dorn. The album was recorded generally live in the studio, around a relentless tour schedule. They spent 300 days on the road in 1970. At Miami Beach Convention Center on 26 August, ex-Cream guitarist Eric Clapton witnessed Duane Allman's skills as a musician for the first time. Clapton was in town recording an album at Criteria, as he relates in his memoir:

> One night, our producer Tom Dowd told me that The Allman Brothers Band was playing the Coconut Grove, and suggested that we all go down to see them. I loved them, but what really blew me away was Duane Allman's guitar-playing. I was mesmerised by him. Tom introduced us to the band after the show, and we invited them back to the studio for a jam, which resulted in me asking Duane to play on the sessions while they were in town. Duane and I became inseparable … he was like the musical brother I'd never had.

The Derek and the Dominos album *Layla and Other Assorted Love Songs* was recorded mostly over the next two weeks, just ahead of the release of *Idlewild South*. Clapton asked Allman to join Derek and the Dominoes full-time. Allman declined but did perform a few times with the band at the end of the year.

The 2015 'Super Deluxe Edition' of *Idlewild South* includes the outtakes 'One More Ride' (also on the *Dreams* box set) and 'Statesboro Blues', remixes of 'In Memory Of Elizabeth Reed' and 'Midnight Rider', the re-recorded single version of 'Revival (Love Is Everywhere)', and nine tracks recorded at Ludlow Garage, Cincinnati on 11 April 1970 (previously released in 1990). This tremendous concert recording includes Duane's only lead vocal on an Allman Brothers song (a version of John Lee Hooker's 'Dimples') and what must be the definitive version of a piece they'd been playing from the very beginning – a reworking of the theme to Donovan's 1967 song 'There Is A Mountain', which they called 'Mountain Jam'.

Just as the album was released, The Allman Brothers Band was filmed in concert at the Fillmore East in New York for a television special called *Welcome To The Fillmore East*. It's available for viewing on YouTube at the time of this writing – the band play tight renditions of 'Don't Keep Me Wonderin'', 'Dreams', 'In Memory Of Elizabeth Reed' and 'Whipping Post'. Equipment malfunctions prevent this from being a perfect record, but to *see* as well as hear the original band performing live over 50 years later, is astounding.

'Revival' (Dickey Betts)

'Revival' was the first original Allman Brothers Band song not written by Gregg Allman. Writer Dickey Betts here introduced an important country influence to the band's: which was to be much more explicit in the forthcoming 'Blue Sky' and 'Ramblin' Man'. The main theme in 'Revival' reminds the listener of The Byrds' 'Jesus Is Just Alright': from their November 1969 album *Ballad Of Easy Rider*. (It was also a minor hit single at the end of that year.)

'Revival' started out as an instrumental, as Betts says: 'We would refer to that first instrumental section of the song as 'The Gypsy Dance'. When I wrote it, I had the image of gypsies dancing around a fire, in my mind, and I tried to conjure that spirit in the music'.

The song opens with Duane Allman's strummed acoustic guitar, followed by bluesy harmonised electric guitar lines. The backing has a swinging Latin feel. Betts said, 'In writing a tune, you have to decide what you are trying to do, and then see if you can make it happen. These are the mental tools I use to help guide me through, to find the proper direction for whatever piece of music I am working on. I used this approach for songs like 'In Memory of Elizabeth Reed', 'High Falls' and 'Revival''.

Rolling Stone enjoyed the track in their December 1970 review: ''Revival' gets things off rousingly, with tambourine and gospel chorus abetting the Duane Allman/Dick Betts multi-guitared attack. The catchy tune suggests a strong single: 'People, can you feel it/Love is everywhere!''.

They were correct. 'Revival' – in a shorter re-recorded arrangement and renamed 'Revival (Love Is Everywhere)' – was released as a single in November 1970 and was the first Allman Brothers single to chart, reaching 92.

'Don't Keep Me Wonderin'' (Gregg Allman)
The live-sounding, in-your-face 'Don't Keep Me Wonderin'' begins with a tight dual slide-guitar-and-harmonica unison lick backed with shifting rhythm interplay from Jaimoe, Butch and Berry. Duane's slide is practically a duet with Gregg's pleading, potent lead vocal.

'Midnight Rider' (Gregg Allman, Robert Kim Payne)
Released as a single, March 1971. Did not chart.

Gregg Allman: ''Midnight Rider' hit me like a damn sack of hoe handles. It was just there, crawling all over me. And about an hour and 15 minutes later, I had the rough draft down... and was putting it down on tape'.

'Midnight Rider' is one of Gregg Allman's signature songs. Amongst his many songs of despair, loss and cheating women, it has a lyric that cuts to the quick:

I've got to run to keep from hiding
And I'm bound to keep on riding
I've got one more silver dollar
But I'm not gonna let 'em catch me, no
Not gonna let 'em catch the Midnight Rider

Band friend and roadie Kim Payne receives was co-writer, as Gregg recalled: 'On 'Midnight Rider', I needed something to start the third verse, and Kim came up with 'I've gone by the point of caring', which was exactly what I needed. 'I've gone by the point of caring' – fuck it – and then, 'Some old bed

29

I'll soon be sharing'. I've got another buck, and I ain't gonna let 'em catch my ass, and then it's just kinda off into the sunset'.

Once the song was written, Allman wanted to record it immediately. As legend has it, he and Payne rounded up Jaimoe and fellow roadie Twiggs Lyndon and broke into Capricorn studios in the middle of the night, recording a rudimentary version with Gregg on 12-string guitar, Lyndon playing elementary bass, and Jaimoe on drums.

Duane Allman and Dickey Betts' subtly sweet guitar work on the final recording, helped create a haunting, simple and perfectly-crafted classic.

British rock singer Joe Cocker released a radically reworked 'Midnight Rider' as a single in 1972. This reached 27 on the *Billboard* Hot 100. The following year, Gregg Allman recorded his own slower and relaxed version on his first solo album, *Laid Back*. This reached 19 in early-1974. Also worth a mention is the reggae version by Jamaican singer Paul Davidson. This gave the song its first and only appearance on the UK singles chart, reaching as high as 10 in early-1976. Please check out Steve Earle's astounding version recorded for *House of Strombo* in 2017. This will make your hair stand on end.

'In Memory Of Elizabeth Reed' (Dickey Betts)

'In Memory Of Elizabeth Reed' resounds like Santana with guts. The twin guitars play tandem, then explode apart (Duane taking the upper register, I think). Brother Greg's comping organ and the rhythm trio set a high-rolling tempo then, and it just goes and goes for a stupendous, and unnoticed, seven minutes. Idlewild South augurs well for the Allmans' future.
Ed Leimbacher, *Rolling Stone*, 24 December 1970

The Allman Brothers' first original instrumental is also their best, and is Dickey Betts' *magnum opus*. The spurious 'southern rock' label was never less appropriate for this band than on this piece, which still sounds fresh, new and miles from anything else in the milieu of popular American music in 1970. Duane Allman told writer Robert Palmer: 'That kind of playing comes from Miles and Coltrane. Particularly *Kind of Blue*. I've listened to that album so many times that for the past couple of years, I haven't hardly listened to anything else'.

Betts explained the song's origins:

'In Memory of Elizabeth Reed' was inspired by a woman I knew named Carmella. At the time, she was involved with a friend of mine (Boz Scaggs), but something started to happen between her and myself. She was a very seductive, sultry, secretive woman, and I thought our little cloak-and-dagger romance was a beautiful image for a song. She and I would rendezvous in this old abandoned graveyard by the river, which was the place I liked to go to write songs. When I wrote this song for her, the gravestone next to where

I was sitting happened to say, 'In Memory of Elizabeth Reed', so that became the song's title ... Berry Oakley and I inspired each other's improvisational creativity while we were in Second Coming. One of our favourite things to do was to jam in minor keys, experimenting freely with the sounds of different minor modes. We allowed our ears to guide us, and this served to inspire the writing of songs like 'In Memory Of Elizabeth Reed'. We were both fascinated with the modal jazz improvisation of Miles Davis and John Coltrane, such as that heard on *Kind of Blue*.

Miles Davis incorporated elements of rock into jazz on tracks such as 'All Blues'. Betts used the opposite approach by using jazz rhythms in a rock instrumental. The two-drummer format and Jaimoe's jazz chops are put to good use. To this, Betts adds harmonised guitar lines in the main theme and throughout: a rock twist on western swing. Betts: 'I first discovered harmonized melodies from listening to ... Bob Wills, where the melodies are harmonized by guitar, pedal steel, piano and violin. Devising harmonized guitar parts became something Duane and I really enjoyed working on together. We would let our imaginations guide us as to what the harmony line should sound like. Of course, the presence of these guitar harmonies became essential to the sound of The Allman Brothers Band'.

The song's power is best appreciated in live recordings, especially the wonderful versions released on *At Fillmore East* and *Wipe the Windows, Check the Oil, Dollar Gas*. 'Liz Reed' remained in the band's live shows from January 1970 until the final shows in October 2014: over 900 known performances.

'Hoochie Coochie Man' (Willie Dixon)
Betts and Oakley drew this Muddy Waters song from their repertoire with their band Second Coming. Waters recorded his much slower original in 1954. The Allmans' version is busy and intense, pushed forward by Oakley's pulsating bass, and that massive percussive backdrop. This is Berry Oakley's only recorded lead vocal. Like his friend Duane Allman, Oakley is not best-remembered as a singer.

'Please Call Home' (Gregg Allman)
Gregg Allman sang this burning blues ballad with power and resonance. It was cut in New York with jazz producer Joel Dorn in two takes. Dorn told writer Randy Poe:

As I remember it, Tommy Dowd was stuck down south and the band was in New York. Tommy said to Duane, 'Look, I can't get up there', and Duane said, 'Well, this is the only time we can record'. So Tommy called me and said, 'Listen, I asked Duane who he wanted to work with, and he said you, so would you do a session with The Allman Brothers?'. I said, 'Of course I would'. It would turn out to be the only chance I ever really had to work with Duane. We did the sessions at Regent Sound, where I did most of my recording. I know we cut two things; we might have done a third. But the only one that made the album was 'Please Call Home'. I just tried to capture what it was that they did. I did the track, and on my résumé I can say I worked with The Allman Brothers. It was just that one cut, but it turned out pretty well.

Gregg's remake on *Laid Back* is majestic.

'Leave My Blues At Home' (Gregg Allman)

The up-tempo 'Leave My Blues at Home', closes the album with hints of jazz funk, some unexpected chord changes and an extended fade-out of the band's signature twin lead guitars. It's songs such as this and 'In Memory Of Elizabeth Reed' that prove that The Allman Brothers Band defy categorisation – they cannot be lumped under the lazy classification of 'southern rock'. Bands such as The Marshall Tucker Band, Molly Hatchet, ZZ Top and Wet Willie – despite their skill as musicians – could never tackle this type of material. Why be constrained by labels?

At Fillmore East (1971)

Personnel:
Duane Allman: lead and slide guitar
Gregg Allman: organ, piano, vocals
Dickey Betts: lead guitar
Jaimoe: drums, congas, timbales
Berry Oakley: bass
Butch Trucks: drums, timpani
Thom Doucette: harmonica on 'Don't Keep Me Wonderin'', 'Done Somebody
Wrong', 'One Way Out', 'Stormy Monday' and 'You Don't Love Me'
Jim Santi: tambourine
Recorded March 1971 at Fillmore East, New York
Producer: Tom Dowd
Release date: July 1971
Chart position: 13

> *At Fillmore East* is the truest fulfilment of Duane Allman's musical vision. The album is an honest look at Duane as an individual artist, and more importantly, as a bandleader. More than just 78 minutes of live improvisational music, the record is the definitive artistic statement of the original Allman Brothers Band.
> **Bob Beatty, *Play All Night! Duane Allman And The Journey To Fillmore East* (2022)**

Between July 1968 and July 1971, being booked at either the Fillmore East in New York City or the Fillmore West in San Francisco was the pinnacle of success for the Woodstock generation of rock bands. Parts or all of many great live albums were recorded at one or the other of these seminal venues – *Wheels of Fire* (Cream, recorded 1968), *The Live Adventures of Mike Bloomfield and Al Kooper* (1969), *Bless Its Pointed Little Head* (Jefferson Airplane, 1969), *Live/Dead* (Grateful Dead, 1969), *Nice* (The Nice, 1969), *The Turning Point* (John Mayall, 1969), *Band of Gypsies* (Jimi Hendrix, 1969), *Mad Dogs & Englishmen* (Joe Cocker, 1970), *At Fillmore: Live at the Fillmore East* (Miles Davis, 1970), *4 Way Street* (Crosby, Stills, Nash & Young, 1970), *The Real Thing* (King Curtis, 1971), *Aretha Live at Fillmore West* (Aretha Franklin, 1971), *Flowers of Evil* (Mountain, 1971), *Performance: Rockin' the Fillmore* (Humble Pie, 1971), *Fillmore East – June 1971* (The Mothers, 1971).
Dickey Betts, in *Rolling Stone*, March 2016:

> Fillmore East was a great-sounding room. It was fun to play. The PA system was set up correctly. It wasn't too loud, it wasn't too soft, and everyone in the room could hear and see.

More than any other recording, it's *At Fillmore East* that secured the legend of The Allman Brothers Band and the Fillmore venues.

The New York Times contested that the band's music was 'blues-based, country-smoothed and laced with bits of jazz and gospel'. And as Randy Poe writes: 'The blues – along with country, gospel and jazz – originated in the south-eastern United States: an area of the country once rife with the oppressed and disenfranchised'. *At Fillmore East* – recorded across five concerts in brash, uptight, cosmopolitan New York City – is the pure distillation of these four key ingredients of American music.

George Kimball wrote in *Rolling Stone* in August 1971 that '(The Allman Brothers) comprise the best damn rock-and-roll band this country has produced in the past five years. And if you think I'm dog-shittin' you, listen to this album'. Gregg Allman had this to say in *Rolling Stone* in March 2016, 'No one did it better in a live setting than the Allman Brothers, and *At Fillmore East* is still the proof, all these years later'. Finally, David McGee in *The Rolling Stone Record Guide* in 1980, remarked that 'There are no wasted notes, no pointless jams, no half-realized vocals – everything counts'.

At Fillmore East was recorded at six shows over the nights of 11, 12 and 13 March 1971 at the 2,654 capacity venue. The Allman Brothers Band were the middle attraction: playing after Elvin Bishop and before Johnny Winter. Recordings from the first night were not used, due to the band employing a horn section which did not gel with the rest of the musicians. Nevertheless, after that 11 March show, the running order was swapped, and The Allman Brothers closed the remaining shows, allowing them to relax into their playing. Bob Beatty wrote in his definitive account of the shows, *Play All Night*, 'At Fillmore East* was a carefully-planned and brilliantly-executed documentation of the band's development. Listeners can hear the closeness of the musicians in their musical conversations, each improvising his part, whether soloing, comping or both simultaneously'.

At Fillmore East was originally planned as a single album including 'Statesboro Blues', 'Done Somebody Wrong', 'Stormy Monday', 'One Way Out', 'Hot 'Lanta' and an edited 'You Don't Love Me'. Wisely expanded to a double set, it retailed at $6.98: the usual cost for a single album.

It went Gold on 25 October 1971. Four days later, Duane Allman was dead. In 2004, the Library of Congress added *At Fillmore East* to its National Recording Registry.

'Statesboro Blues' (Blind Willie McTell)
Recorded 13 March 1971: first show
'Okay, the Allman Brothers Band'. This low-key announcement from the Fillmore's stage manager Michael Ahern opens an album that's consistently catalogued as one of the greatest live albums of the rock era.

'Statesboro Blues' is a tight, punchy kickoff: a perfect opening track on what became the band's breakthrough album. Gregg Allman: 'If we did things right, we could grab people with the first eight bars of a song, and we wouldn't have to worry about the rest of the night. The key was getting them right away'.

'Statesboro Blues' – a wonderful example of an attention grabber – was written by American blues guitarist Blind Willie McTell, who first recorded the song in 1928. Taj Mahal's full-band version – with slide guitar by Jesse Ed Davis – for Mahal's eponymous 1968 debut, was a big influence. Statesboro is 120 miles east of Macon.

The Allman Brothers' version is mostly a showcase for Duane's slide guitar – his soaring, dramatic playing on the intro, grabs you from the very first note. Gregg grunts and Dickey tries to keep up with Duane's astounding playing.

The lock-tight drummers play the interlocking Allman Shuffle: the tight play-off between Trucks' extravagent timekeeping and Jaimoe's jazz flourishes.

'Statesboro Blues' is raw energy from a band of incredible musicians at the peak of their first phase.

'Done Somebody Wrong' (Clarence Lewis, Bobby Robinson, Elmore James)
Recorded 12 March 1971: second show

This was one of the first songs the teenage Allman brothers learned in Daytona Beach – taught to them by local musician Hank Moore. Duane's clean slide tone and the sharply-accented rhythm section, kick the song off, with solos by – in order – Thom Doucette (1:22-2:02), Dickey Betts (2:02-2:42) and a virtuosic Duane Allman (3:08-3:30 and 4:00-4:25). It's a straight blues, but played with a surprising light touch. 'Aw, play the blues', Gregg says. And how.

'Stormy Monday' (T-Bone Walker)
Recorded 13 March 1971: second show (edited)

> While we're doing that blues thing, we're going to play this old Bobby Bland song for you. Actually, it's a T-Bone Walker song.
> Duane Allman introducing 'Stormy Monday' on *At Fillmore East*.

This song was a hit for both Bobby Bland *and* T-Bone Walker. Walker was a pioneering Texas blues guitarist, and 'Call It Stormy Monday (But Tuesday Is Just as Bad)' (the correct title) reached number 5 on *Billboard*'s race chart in 1947. The guitar-playing is astounding. Bobby 'Blue' Bland's soul-blues cover – listed as 'Stormy Monday Blues' – dates from November 1961. It reached five on the R&B chart and 43 on the pop chart. Credit here to Wayne Bennett's jazz-blues guitar-playing. Bland's arrangement uses a minor-chord progression, which the Allmans adapted to great effect: firstly with Hour Glass and later with the Allman Brothers Band.

Randy Poe wrote in *Skydog* in 2006:

> The Allman Brothers' performance of 'Stormy Monday' on At Fillmore East simply took the song away from Bobby 'Blue' Bland and made it theirs and theirs alone. Duane (sans slide) starts the song alone on guitar for four

measures before Dickey and the rest of the band join in for an intro that extends the length of a full verse prior to Gregg's vocal entrance. While Gregg sings the first three verses of the song, Duane and Dickey trade blues licks. At the end of the third verse, Duane takes off on a solo filled with glissandos and bent strings.

Starting with a treacly, slow tempo, Duane pulls out a guitar solo of such grace and beauty (3:34 to 5:12), that ranks as one of the greatest moments in the band's history. His bending technique is masterful. The last few bars sound like he's using a slide.

At 5:12, the track shifts to a jazz-waltz feel for Gregg's pulsating organ showpiece. Never a maestro on the instrument, Gregg nevertheless displays a keen technique, playing with passion and spirit. The tempo drops again for Dickey Betts' electrifying solo (6:02-7:38) which has a light touch that many more-skilful players couldn't emulate. Both Duane and Dickey display their mastery of the blues on this track.

A careful tape edit removed a harmonica solo by Thom Doucette. This was restored in the 1992 release *The Fillmore Concerts*.

Whilst the Duane Allman/Dickey Betts take is surely the definitive rendition of the song, the version with Eric Clapton, Warren Haynes and Derek Trucks -from *The Beacon Box* (2009) – is equally good.

'You Don't Love Me' (Willie Cobbs)

Recorded 13 March 1971: first show (first 7 minutes); 12 March 1971: second show (final 12 minutes)

This was written and recorded by American blues musician Willie Cobbs in 1960. It's a rewrite of Bo Diddley's 'She's Fine, She's Fine' from 1955. The Allmans' version is based on a 1965 recording by Junior Wells and Buddy Guy, perhaps with some influence from the highly successful *Super Session* album by Al Kooper and Stephen Stills (1968).

The *At Fillmore East* recording stretches to 20 minutes, allowing Duane and Dickey to trade solos with Thom Doucette's harmonica. Seven minutes in, the music drops away, and Duane ad libs a two-minute unaccompanied improvisation which exemplifies his phenomenal skill and invention. The drummers kick back in, to back Betts' inspired solo.

Betts said later:

What you hear was played in the spur of the moment, which is exactly what the blues is all about. You have to be fast on your feet, and react instantly to all of the sounds around you, allowing the music to happen in as spontaneous a way as possible. Everything Duane and I play on the extended ending of that track was completely improvised. I played a piece of an old gospel song, some train sounds and things like that, and Duane picked up on those things and went off into his own improvisations.

Gregg Allman:

My brother, he was the bandleader on stage. He'd count it off to start a song, and we would end it when he raised his hand. But in between, the band just let itself go wherever the music would take us.

Galadrielle Allman:

The *Fillmore East* record is a jubilant and vital document of what made The Allman Brothers such special live performers. The album retains the spontaneity of the playing as it happened; it feels like it is unfolding as you listen. The songs are so complex, so varied, that you can hear new moments with every listen. Duane's solo in the centre of 'You Don't Love Me' – played without accompaniment – ends in a long, drawn-out note, stretched to its tense extreme, then another that resolves perfectly. When Twiggs heard the album, he said, 'Those were the two finest notes Duane ever played'.

Randy Poe wrote:

Towards the end, a voice from the audience calls out, 'Play all night!'. It is one of the defining moments in rock – a single jubilant fan caught up in the excitement of the greatest live rock concert ever captured on tape, expressing the feelings of an entire audience.

If you don't think this recording of 'You Don't Love Me' is the ultimate display of a world-class band, then an even better version – from 26 August 1971 and interpolating King Curtis' 'Soul Serenade' – can be heard on the *Dreams* box set (1989) and *Live from A&R Studios* (2016).

'Hot 'Lanta' (Duane Allman, Gregg Allman, Dickey Betts, Butch Trucks, Berry Oakley, Jai Johanny Johanson)
Recorded 13 March 1971: second show
Conceived as a group composition in the Big House in Macon, 'Hot 'Lanta' is a brisk and edgy instrumental with a jazz-waltz feel. Berry Oakley provides an insistent bass line, Gregg excels on the Hammond, and Duane and Dickey play harmonised lead-guitar melodies.
  The song title is allegedly a nickname for the city of Atlanta, though some sources suggest it was the name of one of the band's groups of welcoming local lady friends.

'In Memory Of Elizabeth Reed' (Dickey Betts)
Recorded 13 March 1971:first show
The studio version of 'Liz Reed' from *Idlewild South* is eclipsed by this magnificent 13-minute version where the band channel their jazz heroes Miles

Davis (in particular *A Kind of Blue*, 1959) and John Coltrane (*My Favourite Things*, 1961; *A Love Supreme*, 1965) into something wholly original. The 'southern rock' label is never more wrong than on this visceral, inventive and unique track.

0:00	Duane's introduction.
0:13	guitar volume swells from Betts, giving the impression of violins.
1:28	the main theme begins to emerge, Duane joining Dickey in a dual lead that sometimes doubles the melody line, sometimes provides a harmony line and occasionally provides a counterpoint.
2:39	the tempo picks up with a Latin rhythm and a second-theme melody.
3:10	Betts plays a pure jazz guitar solo around the chords of the second theme. Trucks and Jaimoe lay down the Allman Shuffle as the solo moves into furious rock changes.
5:40	a short reprise of the main theme, leading to a long funky-blues organ solo from Gregg Allman, with very tight accompaniment from the rest of the band.
7:47	Duane lets loose. Berry Oakley adds strong counterpoint on bass.
8:42	the dynamics drop, then build up once more, with Allman reaching a ferocious peak at 10:27.
10:45	another drop in dynamics, with Duane hitting some astounding delicate licks on slide guitar, letting rip again from 11:44.
12:06	the band repeat the main theme before a short percussion break.
12:24	recap of the second theme, abruptly finishing the performance.

This version is so tight, inventive and powerful, that there's a moment of awed silence before the audience goes nuts.

'Whipping Post' (Gregg Allman)
Recorded 13 March 1971: second show
This monster version of 'Whipping Post' fills the whole of side four. The first ten minutes are a more-or-less straight reading of the studio version. Butch Trucks: 'Once the song started, you climbed in and there was no tomorrow, no yesterday; you were just totally in the moment from the time it started to the time it ended'. Ten minutes in, it breaks down into a remarkable free-form improvised section. At 11:26, Betts quotes the main riff from 'Les Brers In A Minor'. From 14:00, the band play a truly awesome and gorgeous chord progression. Trucks:

We're just doodling around, letting go, and then all of a sudden, he starts playing this melody, and you can hear Berry and Gregg and Duane all feeling around for where this chord progression is, because we'd never done this before. By about the second or third progression through, Berry and Duane had locked into what the chord progression was, and then Dickey really laid into it and it just fucking took off. Then when we came roaring back in with the 'Whipping Post' theme again, the place just exploded. We had just paid a visit to a place we'd never been before.

Gregg howls the final chorus, and you expect the song to end. But no, the notes from 'Frere Jacques' signify a slow single-chord exposition lasting four minutes, which builds to a repeat of Gregg's passionate 'Oh, sometimes I feel like I'm dying', echoed by Duane's effortless slide-guitar touch.

Galadrielle Allman: 'One of my favourite games is listening to one instrument at a time. Follow Berry from his solo in 'Whipping Post' through the rest of the song. Just stay with him, pushing the guitars into the periphery. You can do it with each man, and it reveals the truth that they were all soloists in shifting moments, surprisingly creative and varied'.

Contemporary Recordings

At Fillmore East was recorded across six shows, two each night on 11, 12 and 13 March, with further recording on 27 June 1971. Many recordings from these concerts have been made available over the years.

Eat a Peach (1972) contains 'Trouble No More' from 12 March (second show), 'Mountain Jam' from 13 March (second show) and 'One Way Out' from 27 June.

Duane Allman: An Anthology (1972) contains 'Don't Keep Me Wonderin'' from 13 March (second show).

The Road Goes On Forever (1975) contains 'Statesboro Blues' from 12 March.

Duane Allman Anthology, Vol. 2 (1988) contains 'Midnight Rider' from 27 June.

The *Dreams* box set (1989) contains 'Drunken Hearted Boy' from 13 March (second show).

The Fillmore Concerts (1992) is a remix of the original album, but with different versions of 'Statesboro Blues' (12 March, second show), 'Hot 'Lanta' (12 March, second show), the live songs from *Eat a Peach*, and two additional tracks – a stinging 'Don't Keep Me Wonderin'' (13 March, first show) and a shaky 'Drunken Hearted Boy' (13 March, second show).

A deluxe edition of *At Fillmore East* (2003) contains the same songs as *The Fillmore Concerts*, with the additional track 'Midnight Rider'.

The deluxe re-release of *Eat a Peach* (2004) contains the whole of the 27 June concert.

Finally, the 6-CD box set *The 1971 Fillmore East Recordings* (2014) includes the complete concerts from 12 March (two shows), 13 March (two shows) and 27 June. There is also a 5.1 mix for die-hards.

Also of considerable interest is a bootleg called *The Gatlinburg Tapes* recorded in April 1971, which includes a 30-minute jam, four sketches of 'Blue Sky' and three versions of John Coltrane's arrangement of Rodgers and Hammerstein's 'My Favourite Things' (from *The Sound of Music*).

Friday, 29 October 1971, Macon, GA

It was quiet in Macon's Memorial chapel that day, but not for long. Hundreds of people – relatives and friends – gathered, talking, crying about something they still could not believe had happened. The band performed that day at the service like they had never done before: blues, with more meaning now than ever.
Richard Albero, *Guitar Player*, May/June 1973

If you do something, you got to be ready to pay those goddamn dues. I dropped three tabs of good red acid on a motorcycle going a hundred miles an hour down the road; no shoes and no helmet on. And, of course, you've got to pay dues for stuff like that.
Duane Allman

Macon is beautiful in the spring, white magnolia blossoms hanging heavily in the trees, fallen pink cherry petals swirling on the cobblestone streets, and new grass growing in so green it hurts to look right at it. The Ocmulgee River and the train tracks run side by side: the twin means for carrying King Cotton to market back in the day. Together they mark the far edge of Roseville Cemetery – a magnificent Ramblin' city of the dead where marble stones rest in the shade of grand old trees.
Galadrielle Allman, *Please Be With Me: A Song For My Father Duane Allman* (2014)

Over the nights of 25, 26 and 27 June 1971, The Allman Brothers Band performed again at the Fillmore East: the last concerts at this famous venue before it was closed. Galadrielle Allman wrote: 'Jonny Podell told me the 29 people who worked the Fillmore East, voted for the bands they wanted to play. They chose The Allman Brothers Band to be the final act. By all accounts, the second night was stunning. The band played for hours, lulling the audience into a waking dream. It was almost four hours before the band finally touched back down'.

Butch Trucks has likewise often cited the 26 June concert as his favourite by the original lineup. He said in 2001:

That was probably the best music this band ever played. We went onstage around two in the morning; went to about eight in the morning: six hours straight. Finished playing, and there was no applause. The place was jam-packed. Not one person clapped. I look out and everybody's got a smile ear to ear. Some guy gets up, opens the door, and the sun comes in. And a New York crowd, they get up and quietly walk out. I remember Duane walking in front of me, dragging his guitar, saying, 'Goddamn! It's like leaving church'. And the tape machines were sitting outside, but they weren't plugged up.

Bill Graham introduced the band on the final night, 27 June:

Over the years that we've been doing this, the introductions are usually very short, and this one's going to be short but a little longer than usual. The last few days we have had the privilege of working with this particular group. In the past year or so, we've had them on both coasts a number of times. In all that time, I've never heard the kind of music that this group plays. And last night, we had the good fortune of putting them on stage at about two-thirty/ three o'clock, and they walked out of here at seven o'clock in the morning. It's not just that they played quantity – and for my amateur ears, in all my life, I've never heard the kind of music that this group plays. The finest contemporary music. We're going to round it off with the best of them all: The Allman Brothers.

That last night included sets by The J. Geils Band, Albert King, and surprise guests Edgar Winter's White Trash, Mountain, The Beach Boys and Country Joe McDonald.

Duane stayed in New York City to record the album *Push Push* with Herbie Mann over two days at Atlantic Studios, then headed back on the road for six nights in Atlantic City, followed by concerts along the eastern seaboard in Florida, Georgia, New York, Virginia, Minnesota and Ohio. After two weeks break in early-August – during which Duane attended King Curtis' funeral in New York – The Allman Brothers' concert schedule resumed through the rest of the summer across the US, including several in California and one in Canada. After a show at the Painters Mill Music Fair in Owings Mills, Maryland, on 17 October 1971, the band took a short holiday after 18 months of being almost continually on the road.

Twelve days later, Duane Allman was dead.

The band were back in Macon for a break. Duane had just returned from New York. On 29 October 1971, Dixie Meadows and Candace Oakley planned a surprise birthday party for Linda Oakley. Duane no longer lived at the Big House with the Oakleys – he and Dixie were now resident on Burton Avenue: a couple of miles west of Vineville. Duane spent the afternoon at the Big House. At around 5.30 p.m., he set off on his modified Harley Davidson, back home to collect presents and a cake. Berry, Dixie and Candace followed him in two cars. Duane headed west on Vineville Avenue, then south onto Pio Nono Avenue. He took a shortcut west along narrow Hillcrest Avenue. As he approached the intersection with Bartlett Street, it seems he swerved to avoid a truck turning in front of him. Galadrielle Allman:

A flatbed truck began to make a wide turn in the middle of the intersection ahead. For a moment, it seemed that Duane could easily make it around the back end of the truck, but when it stopped short, he was forced under the hot, spinning body of his Harley, and knocked unconscious. Candy and Dixie leaped from their cars and ran to him, calling out for help. Candy banged on the doors of several houses on the street, pleading for someone to call an ambulance. She pulled the covers off the seats of her car to cover him while they waited for help to come. He had a scratch on his face, but the worst of his injuries did not show. It took forever for the ambulance to come, its siren blaring.

Duane was taken to the Medical Centre of Central Georgia: two and a half miles away. Berry had taken a different route to Burton Avenue, and was waiting there when Candace arrived to tell him the news. She called Gregg, who sprinted to the medical centre to attend to his brother.

Duane Allman died of massive internal injuries, after three hours of emergency surgery. He was 24 years old.

Galadrielle Allman, *Please Be With Me: A Song For My Father Duane Allman* (2014):

The whole scene is dissected at great length, to what end? My father was killed in an accident – a meaningless, blameless moment that could never be changed. What else is there to know?

The memorial service at 3 p.m. on 1 November 1971 included the surviving Allman Brothers Band performing 'The Sky Is Crying', 'Key To The Highway', 'Stormy Monday', 'In Memory Of Elizabeth Reed' and 'Statesboro Blues'. Gregg – still just 23 – sang 'Melissa' alone with his acoustic guitar. Jerry Wexler gave the eulogy:

It was at King Curtis' funeral that I last saw Duane Allman, and Duane with tears in his eyes told me that Curtis' encouragement and praise was valuable to him in the pursuit of his music and career. They were both gifted natural musicians with an unlimited ability for truly melodic improvisation. They were both born in the south, and they both learned their music from great black musicians and blues singers. They were both utterly dedicated to their music, and both intolerant of the false and the meretricious, and they would never permit the incorporation of the commercial compromise to their music: not for love or money. Those of us who were privileged to know Duane, will remember him from all the studios, backstage dressing rooms, the Downtowners, the Holiday Inns, the Sheratons, the late nights, relaxing after the sessions, the whisky and the music talk, playing back cassettes until night gave way to dawn, the meals and the pool games, and fishing in Miami and Long Island – this young beautiful man who we love so dearly but who is not lost to us, because we have his music, and the music is imperishable.

Duane was buried in Roseville Cemetery in Macon. Willie Perkins: 'Rumours that he was provided a joint in his pocket and a slide bottle on his finger for his final journey, are not untrue'.

Galadrielle Allman:

His spark set their fire. He was their driving wheel. Losing him, irrevocably changed everyone who knew him, and literally changed the way the world felt to all of us. It seemed impossible that someone who lived so fiercely and with such hunger for all that life could offer, could be taken so suddenly.

Cameron Crowe tells a story of how Gregg was affected by his brother's death in *The Day The Music Died*:

I first met The Allman Brothers Band in 1973. I was 16, and it was my first major assignment for *Rolling Stone* magazine. After ten days on the road with the group, I'd seen every show and taped long interviews with everyone. The band's publicist had said in advance that the tragic motorcycle death of Duane Allman was a subject not to be discussed, but every interview and every conversation had eventually turned back to that sad topic. They were pained and heartfelt interviews, and I was amazed that the band and crew had been so open with me. The night before I was to leave the tour and write the story, my hotel phone rang. I was sharing the room with photographer Neal Preston, and Neal picked up the phone. He mumbled a few sentences in a low nervous voice. I instantly knew something was wrong. 'Gregg wants you to come to his room', he said. 'He wants you to bring him all your interview tapes, right now'. A cold fear crept through me. Gregg Allman had been friendly to me, but many others had warned that he was distant and moody. I wondered about the possible psychology of such a close-knit group as The Allman Brothers: an outsider had killed Duane; now another outsider wanted to write about it. I gathered all but one of the 15 interview tapes, and headed upstairs to Allman's room. I still remember shaking so hard that I dropped the tapes in the elevator. Allman answered the door himself. He was solemn; his long blond hair was pressed against his head with perspiration. His eyes were fixed on some distant point as he led me inside. 'Let me see your ID', he said. 'You could be anybody, hanging around, asking us questions. We told you everything. It's all on those cassettes'. He looked over to an empty chair across the room. I clenched my teeth together to keep them from chattering. 'Duane's in the room right now. He's sitting there and he's laughing at you'.

Duane Allman's tenure within the band that bore his name lasted 31 months. Jon Landau in *Real Paper*:

(Duane) had literally flirted with death too often to be surprised. No matter how briefly you knew him or how little, the more you got to know him, the more you realized that underneath the energy, the humour, the mock arrogance and the real arrogance, was a troubled man who knew just how talented he was, but who didn't know how to live at peace with that talent. In some ways, the world wasn't ready for him. And in others, he just wasn't ready for *it.*

In *Rolling Stone*'s 13 April 1972 edition, Tony Glover noted: 'Sometimes it all seems to come down to the question of survival, and learning to live with loss. Rock and blues have lost a lot of people in the past five years, but the death of an artist always diminishes the music more than the death of a *star* – and Duane Allman was an artist. He lived for and in music, loving it with the kind of possessed passion that sometimes leads people to believe that bluesmen have traded their souls to the Devil for the magic of their music'.

Eat a Peach (1972)

Personnel:
Duane Allman: slide and lead guitar, acoustic guitar (except on 'Ain't Wastin' Time No More', 'Les Brers In A Minor' and 'Melissa')
Gregg Allman: lead vocals, Hammond organ, piano, Fender Rhodes, acoustic guitar
Dickey Betts: lead guitar, lead vocals on 'Blue Sky'
Jaimoe: drums, congas
Berry Oakley: bass
Butch Trucks: drums, percussion, timpani, gong, vibes, tambourine
Recorded 12/13 March and 27 June 1971, Fillmore East, New York; September-December 1971, Criteria Studios, Miami, Florida
Producer: Tom Dowd
Release date: February 1972
Chart position: 4

Shall I part my hair behind?
Do I dare to eat a peach?
I shall wear white flannel trousers and walk upon the beach
I have heard the mermaids singing, each to each
I do not think that they will sing to me
T. S. Eliot, *The Love Song of J. Alfred Prufrock*, 1915

Whenever I'm in Georgia, I eat a peach for peace ... the two-legged Georgia variety.
Duane Allman

One of their first gigs after the tragedy was Thanksgiving night at Carnegie Hall. The trademark dual guitar harmonies and interplay were missing – but the band still boogied hard, strong and soaring. It was as if each of the five had expanded some to fill the empty space, and a different kind of internal structure started to grow.
Tony Glover, *Rolling Stone*, 3 April 1972

Eat A Peach For Peace – as this album was initially called (based on Duane's stock answer to any interviewer asking what the band were doing to end the Vietnam War) – was always planned as a part-live/part-studio album. Three songs had been recorded with Duane – Gregg's 'Stand Back' (co-written with Berry Oakley), Betts' bright 'Blue Sky' and Duane's acoustic 'Little Martha'.

The band returned to the studio at the end of 1971. Gregg wrote later, 'We knew we had to get back in the studio and we had to get back on the road, because keeping busy was the only way to avoid going crazy. I knew that, but that's about all I knew. We had to keep going, because I didn't want to think about my brother – or anything, for that matter'.

The band recorded three new songs in the last weeks of 1971: 'Ain't Wastin' Time No More', 'Les Brers In A Minor' and 'Melissa'. These were placed together on side one of *Eat A Peach*. Gregg wrote: 'Those last three songs, they just kinda floated right on out of us. They proved that the music hadn't died with my brother'.

With selections from the band's Fillmore East concerts representing their 1971 concerts with Duane, *Eat A Peach* hedged its bets, with three sides of *old* and one side of *new*. It was the band's first top-10 album. Gregg said, 'We'd been through hell, but somehow we were rolling bigger than ever'.

The band played the entire album in order, at the third Peach Festival in Scranton, PA, in August 2014.

'Ain't Wastin' Time No More' (Gregg Allman)
Released as a single, April 1972. Chart position: 77
The album's opening track and lead single was the band's first new music following Duane Allman's untimely death. Most of the music was complete before Duane died, and the lyrics were written shortly after the accident. It works as both an acknowledgement of mortality, and a reason for carrying on.

Last Sunday morning, the sunshine felt like rain
The week before, they all seemed the same
With the help of God and true friends, I've come to realize
I still have two strong legs, and even wings to fly

Gregg said in 2006:

'After my brother's accident, we had three vinyl sides done of *Eat A Peach*, so I thought, well, we'll do that, and then I wrote 'Ain't Wastin' Time No More'. I wrote that for my brother. We were all in pretty bad shape. I had just gotten back from Jamaica, and I was weighing at about 156, 6ft.1 and a half: I was pretty skinny. So we went back down there, got in the studio and finished the record. And the damn thing shipped gold'.

Gregg Allman's heartfelt composition captures – in part – his feelings at one of the most difficult times of his life. His rock-solid piano playing drives the song, supplemented by Jaimoe's gently-flowing percussion, and the lyrical guitar-playing of Dickey Betts: playing slide for the first time.

'Les Brers In A Minor' (Dickey Betts)

An instrumental excursion that sounds like Dickey OD-ing on *Live/Dead*.
Robert Christgau

The title is mangled French for 'The Brothers In A Minor', and is an atmospheric nine-minute instrumental, very much in a Santana-meets-Grateful

Dead mood, with clever elements of jazz harmony. It was first introduced to the band's setlist in January 1972, and became a regular for the next four years, sometimes stretching out for 30 minutes or more.

After a free-form opening which swells and moves around different chords, the song kicks into first gear at 3:47. Berry Oakley's bass line is prominent. The main theme is extrapolated from a lick Dickey Betts played in live versions of 'Whipping Post' (listen at 11:21 on *At Fillmore East*). Dickey and Gregg work through the twists and turns, over a rich, syncopated percussion groove. An inventive bridge section interrupts the flow at 4:25 as we move into five minutes of inspired open-ended soloing and jamming.

Tony Glover wrote in *Rolling Stone on* 3 April 1972:

'Les Brers In A Minor' is a masterpiece. It's a highly cinematic-sounding – almost symphonically-majestic – construction. It begins with two long and rising suspensions of swirling sound, which make for a lot of mind movies, and the credits start to roll as bass and congas begin a popping riff, joined by a guitar line that is maddeningly familiar. A soaring, nearly-two-octave ascending scale explodes the song – it starts to drive with the same kind of midnight highway-riding power riffs that characterized 'In Memory Of Elizabeth Reed'.

'Melissa' (Gregg Allman)
Released as a single, August 1972. Chart position: 86

'Melissa' is a powerful acoustic song, played tenderly but with much feeling. Gregg Allman spoke at length about this song in an interview with the *San Luis Obispo Tribune* in November 2006, and repeated the story in his memoir:

I wrote that song in 1967 in a place called the Evergreen Hotel in Pensacola, Florida. By that time, I got so sick of playing other people's material that I just sat down and said, 'Okay, here we go. One, two, three – we're going to try to write songs'. And about 200 songs later – much garbage to take out – I wrote this song called 'Melissa'. I just started strumming it and hit these beautiful chords. It was just open strings, then an E shape, first fret, then moved to the second fret. This is a great example of the way different tunings can open up different roads to you as a songwriter. The music immediately made me feel good, and the words just started coming to me. And I had everything but the title – I thought, 'But back home, we always run... to sweet Barbara: no. Diane? We always run... to sweet Bertha'. No, so I just kind of put it away for a while. So one night I was in the grocery store – it was my turn to go get the tea, the coffee, the sugar and all that other shit – and there was this Spanish lady there, and she had this little toddler with her, this little girl. And I'm sitting there, getting a few things and what have you. And this little girl takes off, running down the aisle. And the lady yells, 'Oh, Melissa! Melissa, come back, Melissa!'. And I went, 'Oh, that's it'.

The first version was recorded during demo sessions for 31st Of February in September 1968, with Butch Trucks and Duane Allman; producer Steve Alaimo was credited as co-writer. The version recorded here for *Eat A Peach* is very similar but warmer and a touch more resigned, perhaps because the song was a particular favourite of Duane Allman. Gregg played the song on one of Duane's old guitars at his funeral, and this is perhaps the reason why only two live performances of 'Melissa' were logged in the 1970s.

Greg's mournful vocals and Oakley's dancing bass are matched by Dickey Betts' terrific lyrical guitar swells: some of his best playing. A gem.

'Mountain Jam' (Donovan Leitch, Duane Allman, Gregg Allman, Dickey Betts, Berry Oakley, Butch Trucks, Jai Johnny Johanson)
Recorded live at the Fillmore East, 13 March 1971: second show

Filling two sides of *Eat A Peach*, this very long instrumental jam was triggered by the flute introduction to the 1967 Donovan song 'There Is A Mountain'. It's entirely possible that Duane borrowed the lick from the Grateful Dead – listen to 'Alligator' on *Anthem Of The Sun*: that same riff appears at around nine minutes in. The version Jerry Garcia played with the Allmans at Watkins Glen in 1973 closely resembles 'Alligator' in tempo and feel.

'Mountain Jam' was part of the band's set from the very beginning. Its first-known performance is from Macon on 4 May 1969, and it's perhaps appropriate that they also played the song at their very last gig, on 28 October 2014.

The *Eat a Peach* recording is a direct continuation of 'Whipping Post' from *At Fillmore East* – you can hear the song begin as 'Whipping Post' – and the album – fades out.

These are the sections from 'Mountain Jam'. Timings are taken from the *Eat a Peach* deluxe-edition CD:

0:00   delicate harmony guitar lines weave around the main theme initially unaccompanied, the band kicks in at 0:23.

2:41   an extraordinarily musical guitar solo from Duane, which moves into overdrive at 3:41 with impeccable rhythm section work from Oakley, Trucks and Jaimoe.

4:41   simple, expressive Hammond organ work from Gregg.

7:20   a long, tough, bluesy guitar solo by Dickey Betts, with phenomenal rhythm-section playing.

10:54   a brief recap around the notes of the main theme, with harmonised guitar lines. The rock arrangement moves to more of a pure jazz feel.

13:12   a furious in-the-pocket tandem drum solo from Butch and Jaimoe.

18:43   an astonishing syncopated bass solo from Berry.

22.11   the guitars re-enter, Duane now playing a sweet slide part.

22:39   the piece shifts to a shuffle, and makes a fleeting reference to Jimi Hendrix' 'Third Stone From The Sun'.

25:55   another wonderful slide guitar solo from Duane.

27:29   transition to a 6/8 instrumental take, based around the chords of 'Will The Circle Be Unbroken?', with expressive slide guitar.

30:14   a reprise of the main theme, leading a powerful conclusion and Duane's band introductions.

There are arguably better performances of 'Mountain Jam' from 1970 (see *Live at Ludlow Garage, Bear's Sonic Journals Live at Fillmore East*, and the New Orleans show from March 1970 released in 2019), but this is the only 1971 show recorded professionally to multitrack. Here is a group fully at ease with each other's musicality.

Initially having been placed across two sides of the vinyl album, the CD of *Eat a Peach* edits both halves together; *The Fillmore Tapes* appends it to 'Whipping Post' for 50 minutes of amazing music.

In September 2014, Jon Dale wrote in *Uncut*:

> At such moments – where Betts and Duane Allman wrestle with each other in space, carving up the air with silvery threads of single-note splurge – The Allman Brothers Band come closest, in some respects, to that other legendary jam band the Grateful Dead. And it's damn curious to measure both groups' live form via recorded reflection. While the Dead may have reinvigorated the Great American Songbook, their performances of blues songs were often perfunctory, hampered by an occasional bloodlessness in the playing. By contrast, this is where the Allman Brothers Band excels: tight, sure-footed and gutsy.

'One Way Out' (Elmore James, Marshall Sehorn, Sonny Boy Williamson II)

Recorded live at the Fillmore East, 27 June 1971. Released as a single, November 1972. Chart position: 86

This snarling blues cover is heavily reworked in the Allmans' style. Williamson's recording with Buddy Guy on the 1965 album *The Real Folk Blues*, features the signature guitar line used on *Eat A Peach*.

Dickey Betts plays the opening riff on this live version recorded at the band's final Fillmore East performance on the night of the venue's closing: 27 June 1971. Duane emulates Sonny Boy's harmonica lick with slide guitar. Betts takes the first solo (at 1:58), driving and loud. At 3:21, Berry Oakley comes in half a beat early, briefly throwing the band off track. Butch and Jaimoe effortlessly turn the rhythm around. This minor wrinkle is an essential part of the track's charm.

'Trouble No More' (Muddy Waters)

Recorded live at the Fillmore East, 12 March 1971: second show

A tough live version of the track from the band's debut album, which remained in their set throughout their career.

'Stand Back' (Gregg Allman, Berry Oakley)

The final three songs on *Eat A Peach* comprise Duane Allman's last studio recordings. Here he is at the absolute peak of his musicianship. The tightly grooving 'Stand Back' – originally titled 'Calico' – is another *bad-woman* song. Duane emulates Miles Davis by only playing where absolutely necessary: his slide solo is sublime.

'Stand Back' features drums by Jaimoe: Butch Trucks added only a minor overdub. He said in 2001: 'I felt like 'Stand Back' was the perfect song for Jaimoe – really funky stuff that he's so good at. I knew that the only way I could get him to do this, was get my ass out of there completely and let him have at it. I finally convinced him to try it, so he did it three or four times. The fifth try is the version on the record'.

'Blue Sky' (Dickey Betts)

Dickey Betts' first lead vocal on an Allman Brothers Band song, was written about his Native Canadian girlfriend Sandy 'Bluesky' Wabegijig. It's a beautiful song with a light touch and a country feel. ''Blue Sky' wasn't *that* country', suggested Betts. 'It could have been done by Poco or the Dead'.

The positivity of 'Blue Sky' (three short verses, a short chorus and a long instrumental section) contrasts with the anguish of many of Gregg Allman's songs. This is exemplified by the reference to the First Christian Church across the street in Macon: in the lines, 'Good old Sunday mornin'/Bells are ringin' everywhere'.

The song was performed as early as August 1971 – a live version from the State University of New York (SUNY) in Stony Brook on 19 September 1971 was released in 2003. Butch Trucks remembers this was the first song recorded for *Eat A Peach* that same month.

Betts said, 'When we originally recorded 'Blue Sky', Duane and I tried all different kinds of harmonies until we found the one that best suited the song. We found that the softer-edged harmony was what worked best'.

The solo section starts at 1:09, with Betts taking the lead, and Allman resolving the chords high on the neck. They switch halfway through at 2:30, as both players harmonise for a few notes before Duane takes the lead. They harmonise again from 4:01 – three minutes of guitar-playing in a five-minute song.

Tony Glover in *Rolling Stone*, 13 April 1972:

'Blue Sky' – though filled with 'running rivers' and 'sunny skies' – has a pure and natural freshness that 10,000 folked-up troubadours will never reach, no matter how much straw they got in their boots. The guitar interplay between Duane and Dickey has a country cleanness, but stays solidly in the throbbing Allman groove – can you dig country/blues in a new kind of marriage?

Betts and Wabegijig married in 1973, and divorced two years later.

'Little Martha' (Duane Allman)

This is a delightful two-Dobro instrumental duet – the first and only songwriting credit for Duane Allman. Despite rumours of the piece being named for a deceased baby with a memorial at Roseville Cemetery, Duane wrote it for a girl with whom he was having an affair: Dixie Lee Meadows. Little Martha was Duane's nickname for her.

Galadrielle Allman:

Duane had an incredible dream. He walked into a men's room in the lobby of a big hotel – like a Holiday Inn – and there was Jimi Hendrix: his wild corona of hair, his purple jacket covered in snaking gold cord and shiny buttons, a long red scarf around his neck. Duane had heard that Jimi died, and wondered if they were in Heaven, and so he asked him, 'Hey man, are you okay?'. But Jimi was excited and waved Duane over to the sink with a smile so big he could see every one of his teeth. 'Man, come take a look at this! It's a groove!'. Jimi bent down toward the silver faucet, turned it gently, and kept teasing and turning, and as he did, a beautiful guitar riff came floating out and bounced off the white tile walls around them. Duane stood with his hands on his hips, and watched Jimi play the pretty little rambling tune by twisting the faucet. (On waking) Duane pulled his Dobro into bed and started picking out the riff. The melody Jimi gave him was the seed of the song 'Little Martha'.

Gregg told *Hittin' The Note* in 2001: 'He used to play stuff like that all the time. ('Little Martha') was just this little lick that he had, and over a period of about four years, I watched him develop it into a beautiful song. There would have been more like it, I'm sure'.

The *Eat A Peach* version has two guitars: both in open-E tuning. A different mix released on the 1989 *Dreams* box set includes Berry Oakley's beautifully-melodic bass part, which was mixed out for *Eat A Peach*. Restored for *Dreams*, this previously unheard component, lifts the song from charming to perfection.

Brothers and Sisters (1973)

Personnel:
Gregg Allman: vocals, Hammond organ, rhythm guitar ('Wasted Words'), backing vocals ('Ramblin' Man')
Dickey Betts: lead guitar, vocals ('Ramblin' Man', 'Pony Boy'), slide guitar ('Wasted Words'), dobro ('Pony Boy')
Jaimoe: drums, congas ('Ramblin' Man', 'Jessica')
Chuck Leavell: piano, backing vocals ('Ramblin' Man'), Fender Rhodes ('Jessica', 'Come And Go Blues')
Berry Oakley: bass ('Wasted Words', 'Ramblin' Man')
Butch Trucks: drums, percussion, timpani ('Jessica'), congas ('Come And Go Blues', 'Jelly Jelly')
Lamar Williams: bass ('Come And Go Blues', 'Jelly Jelly', 'Southbound', 'Jessica', 'Pony Boy')
Les Dudek: co-lead guitar ('Ramblin' Man'), acoustic guitar ('Jessica')
Tommy Talton: acoustic guitar ('Pony Boy')
Recorded October-December 1972 at Capricorn Sound, Macon, Georgia
Producers: Johnny Sandlin and The Allman Brothers Band
Release date: August 1973
Chart positions: UK: 42, US: 1

If losing Duane Allman in a motorcycle accident in October 1971 didn't end the band, then the double whammy of Berry Oakley dying in almost identical circumstances, surely would. Gregg Allman: 'The truth is that Berry Oakley's life ended when my brother's life did. Never have I seen a man collapse like that, though I would never use the word 'weak' when talking about Berry Oakley. He just couldn't continue on without my brother. Maybe Duane was the brother he never had, but whatever it was, the loss of Duane was too much for him'. Dickey Betts agreed: 'Berry took it hard. But we all took it hard'.

Oakley had been seriously depressed over the previous year, and roadie Joe Dan Petty had even replaced Oakley for live gigs from time to time. But the addition of pianist Charles 'Chuck' Leavell in September 1972 gave Oakley impetus to work. Leavell, interviewed by the *Atlanta Business Chronicle* in 2015:

I came to Macon for the first time in 1969, to investigate Capricorn Records. I was really blown away with what I saw. I decided to come there permanently, or at least give it a try, so I moved there in 1970 and began working my way up the ladder. I ended up in a couple of bands that quite often opened concerts for the Allmans. I always insisted on an acoustic piano for our sets, and then our equipment would be pulled back and the Allman Brothers would set up and play. Some of the guys in our band would go back to the hotel room or go off to do whatever, but I always liked to hang around and hear the Allmans play. I'd sit there at the piano backstage, and while the Allmans were doing their concert, I'd play along. By doing that, I got familiar with a lot of their tunes. By 1972, I was asked to play on Greg Allman's solo record, *Laid Back*, and in that process, there were these jam sessions that went on that included the other Allman Brothers. After about three weeks of this, I was called into a meeting (with Phil Walden and the band) and asked if I would join. The band had been out as a five-piece for some time, to fulfil some obligations. As you can imagine, it was a very difficult and emotional time. After a little break, and doing Greg's solo record and asking me to join, things went in another direction. I would like to think it was a good decision.

As Randy Poe wrote: 'The decision was... a stroke of genius'.
The band – now again a six-piece – performed at Hofstra University in Hempstead, New York on 2 November 1972. Two new songs were added to the setlist: 'Wasted Words' and 'Ramblin' Man'. Returning to Capricorn Sound in Macon, these were the first two songs the band recorded for their fifth album. Both feature Oakley and Leavell.
Berry Oakley died on 11 November 1972. Jaimoe told *Hittin' the Note* editor John Lynskey:

Berry started getting really, really messed up. He was having a rough time with himself because he didn't know what to do with the whole situation. It just ate him up, man. We didn't know what was happening with Berry. We didn't know if he was going nuts or what. He was drinking, like, two-fifths of vodka a day – crazy stuff like that. He was really disturbed about what was going on, and he missed Duane so much. And then, a couple of weeks later, the accident happened.

Randy Poe wrote in *Skydog* in 2006:

Chuck was driving toward the Big House, Berry was on his Triumph 750 motorcycle, going east on Napier Avenue. (Roadie) Kim Payne was riding next to him. They were on their way to the Big House as well. Berry and Kim were playing around on their bikes, one passing a car on the right side while the other passed it on the left. Going east on Napier Avenue, there is a sharp curve to the right just as one approaches Inverness Avenue. As Berry was nearing Inverness, a city bus was heading west on Napier. The driver saw that the motorcycle was on his side of the road. Even though the bus driver swerved to his right and hit the brakes, Berry failed to lean far enough into the curve to avoid hitting the side of the bus. The impact was so severe that he was thrown almost 60 feet down Inverness. The momentum of the Triumph as it bounced off the side of the bus sent it in the same direction, and it landed right on top of Oakley: precisely what had happened to Duane. When Kim Payne got to Berry, he found the external damage to be minimal. The bassist's nose was bleeding, and his helmet was cracked. Berry was able to stand up. Being less than a mile and a half from the Big House, he decided to catch a ride home rather than go to the hospital. A short time later, says Chuck Leavell, 'Red Dog and some of the other guys were bringing Berry down the stairs, and he was in obvious agony and pain. They told me, 'We've got to get him to the hospital.' I said, 'Let's go.' We loaded him in my station wagon and got him to the hospital as quickly as we could.' Oakley was admitted to the hospital a few minutes before 3:00 p.m. He was pronounced dead less than an hour later. He had been mortally injured the moment the accident happened.

Berry Oakley died one year and 13 days after Duane Allman. The two accidents took place within four blocks of each other. Like Allman, Oakley was 24 years old. 'Berry really died of a broken heart', suggests Bob Beatty.

At Berry's memorial service at Hart's Mortuary in Macon, the band played 'Hoochie Coochie Man', 'Wasted Words' and 'Liz Reed'. His grave is beside Duane's at Roseville Cemetery in Macon. Oakley's secret girlfriend from California – Julia Densmore – was four-months pregnant with their son: who came to be named Berry Duane Oakley.

The band decided to carry on and, after some auditions, recruited Jaimoe's high-school friend Lamar Williams as their bassist. Jaimoe explained in 1997: 'Lamar was the third bassist to audition. We played about two or three songs and everyone was like, 'Wow, man'. And Butch told all of us 'We've found our bass player'. Everyone agreed'. Williams – a brilliant musician – was performing live with the band by the end of November. Over the following few weeks, this new lineup recorded the rest of the new album *Brothers and Sisters*: starting with 'Come And Go Blues'.

Early in January 1973, Berry Oakley's widow Linda was evicted from the Big House after almost three years residency.

The eye-catching *Brothers and Sisters* album cover is a photograph of Butch Trucks' son Vaylor. The back cover features Berry Oakley's daughter Brittany. The inner sleeve pictures the band and road crew's extended family.

Brothers and Sisters sold over 1,000,000 copies within a month of release, and spent five weeks at the top of the *Billboard* album charts. It was also the band's only album to enter the UK charts: managing just three weeks in October 1973.

A 2013 super-deluxe edition expands the album to four CDs, including the band's complete Winterland concert on 26 September 1973, and a disc of 'rehearsals, jams and outtakes'. This latter disc has alternative takes of 'Wasted Words' and 'Southbound', rehearsals of 'Trouble No More', 'One Way Out' and 'Done Somebody Wrong' (seemingly the only available studio versions of the last two), a mighty version of 'I'm Gonna Move To The Outskirts Of Town', the first version of 'Jelly Jelly' ('Early Morning Blues'), and two otherwise-unheard songs – a unique and excellent Allman/Leavell composition called 'Double Cross', and the incredible 16-minute studio improvisation 'A Minor Jam' which is credited to Chuck Leavell, Lamar Williams, Jaimoe, Butch Trucks and guitarist Les Dudek.

Two other albums should be mentioned here. *Beginnings* is a 1973 double re-release of *The Allman Brothers Band* and *Idlewild South*. The debut album was remixed by Tom Dowd, replacing Adrian Barber's original mix. This removed the reverb from Gregg Allman's lead vocals. Also of particular note, 'It's Not My Cross To Bear' fades out about ten seconds later on *Beginnings*, but loses the short reprise heard in the 1969 mix; the 1973 remix of 'Every Hungry Woman' has a previously unheard hi-hat in the introduction, and fades around ten seconds later; 'Dreams' has a different stereo balance of the instrumentation, and, finally, the closing notes of 'Whipping Post' removes the fade-out, so it comes to a cold stop. *Beginnings* was released in February 1973, and was a big success: certified Gold for sales of 500,000 copies by the end of the year. Note that 'Dreams' is listed as 'Dreams I'll Never See' on this re-release.

Gregg Allman's solo album *Laid Back*, dates from October 1973 and includes a new version of 'Midnight Rider' with an orchestral arrangement. This was released as a single, reaching 19 in early-1974. *Laid Back* itself went Gold and reached number 13.

'Wasted Words' (Gregg Allman)

'I ain't no saint, and you sure as hell ain't no saviour'

The classic 'Wasted Words' was first recorded by Gregg Allman as a demo for his *Laid Back* album. This sparse but driving version – which features Johnny Winter, Buddy Miles and Berry Oakley – is available on the out-of-print 1997 compilation *One More Try: An Anthology*. Dickey Betts plays slide guitar on the album version, very much copying the feel of Johnny Winter's playing on the demo. Chuck Leavell's presence is immediately obvious with his barrelhouse piano-playing – it's low in the mix but adds a rollicking counterpoint to the ultra-tight rhythm section. The band really rocks in the last minute. Lovely stuff.

A half-hearted rehearsal of 'Wasted Words' is included in the 2013 super-deluxe edition of *Brothers And Sisters*.

'Ramblin' Man' (Dickey Betts)
Released as a single, August 1973. Chart position: 2

At their best – 'Ramblin' Man': a miraculous revitalization of rock's earliest conceit – they just may be the best.
Robert Christgau

When 'Ramblin' Man' became a hit, everything changed.
Dickey Betts

Dickey Betts' hit paydirt with a song he wrote as an homage to the 1951 Hank Williams song of the same name. 'Ramblin' Man' is The Allman Brothers Band's most commercially-successful song. A catchy five-second introduction heralds a radio-friendly chorus, a later chorus with a memorable three-note fanfare, and liquid guitar lines.

My father was a gambler down in Georgia
And he wound up on the wrong end of a gun
And I was born in the back seat of a Greyhound bus
Rollin' down Highway 41

That colourful opening verse references Route 41, which runs from Florida to Michigan, passing through Macon, a few blocks from the Big House where the song was written. It joins a long line of classic songs about restlessness or the inability to stay in one place too long – 'Leaving On A Jet Plane', 'Carolina In My Mind', 'Marrakesh Express', 'Kathmandu', 'Proud Mary', 'America', 'On The Road Again', 'King Of The Road' and many others.

Betts told author Marc Myers: 'When I was a kid, my dad was in construction and used to move the family back and forth between central Florida's east and west coasts. I'd go to one school for a year and then the other the next. I had two sets of friends, and spent a lot of time in the back seat of a Greyhound bus. We needed one more song for *Brothers and Sisters*, and I said, 'Well, I got this song''.

'Ramblin' Man' ends with an intricate two-guitar playout inspired by the end of Derek and the Dominos' 'Layla'. Betts said: 'I added that long ending to it in the studio, to try and take it away from being a straight country song'. After trying to overdub several guitar parts himself, he ultimately recruited his friend Les Dudek to play lead with him, employing the twin-guitar harmony sound Betts had forged with Duane Allman.

The band played 'Ramblin' Man' on the premiere of a TV show called *In Concert*: recorded on 2 November 1972. It was their first national TV appearance and Berry Oakley's last performance. The show aired after his death and was dedicated to him. Almost a year later – 5 October 1973 – The Allman Brothers Band performed 'Ramblin' Man' on *Don Kirchner's Rock Concert*. The following week, the song peaked at number 2 on the *Billboard* Hot 100. It was kept from number one by Cher's 'Half Breed'. For the record, the rest of an incredibly strong top 10 that week comprised 'Let's Get It On' (Marvin Gaye), 'Higher Ground' (Stevie Wonder), 'Angie' (The Rolling Stones), 'That Lady' (The Isley Brothers), 'Loves Me Like A Rock' (Paul Simon), 'Midnight Train To Georgia' (Gladys Knight & the Pips), 'Keep On Truckin'' (Eddie Kendricks) and 'We're An American Band' (Grand Funk).

'Ramblin' Man' represented not only a stylistic change in direction for the band (Betts' country-pop flavour would now be a major part of their output), but also a shift in power. Betts' hit put him – finally – on an equal footing with Gregg Allman. As Allman's drink/drugs abuse increased, that balance continued to move in the years to come.

'Come And Go Blues' (Gregg Allman)

This first song recorded after Berry Oakley's death could've worked on the band's debut. Originally written on acoustic guitar in open-G tuning (and occasionally performed that way in later concerts), 'Come And Go Blues' is built around a beautiful descending blues turnaround, over a constant thrumming bass. Lamar Williams' skill as a player, anchors the track, Gregg delivers a committed vocal, and we are treated to tasteful solos from Leavell and Betts.

Gregg Allman re-recorded the song for his 1977 solo album *Playin' Up A Storm*.

'Jelly Jelly' (Billy Eckstine, Earl Hines)

Gregg's showcase on the album is a murky blues written and recorded by jazz bandleader Earl Hines, with 'vocal refrain' by co-writer Billy Eckstine, in December 1940. It was the B-side to the 10" single 'I'm Falling For You' the following year. The Allmans took their arrangement from Bobby 'Blue' Bland's 1962 version. As with 'Stormy Monday', they attach some additional chord changes, to give the song their own twist. Chuck Leavell plays a terrific piano solo that no doubt would've delighted both Bobby Bland and Earl Hines.

Intriguingly, a *Brothers And Sisters* outtake released in 2013 uses exactly the same backing track but with different vocals and lyrics: 'Early Morning Blues' is credited to Gregg Allman and extends for four minutes beyond the fade-out of 'Jelly Jelly'.

According to Johnny Sandlin's book *A Never-Ending Groove*, Gregg was in bad shape and couldn't finish the lyrics to 'Early Morning Blues'. Instead, he sang 'Jelly Jelly' over the backing track. Either way, the backing track draws heavily on Bobby Bland's version of the Eckstine/Hines song. This was evidently a last-minute change – some pressings of the album's inner sleeve list 'Early Morning Blues' (and print the lyrics) in place of 'Jelly Jelly'.

'Southbound' (Dickey Betts)

Written on the tour bus between gigs, 'Southbound' is an up-tempo Dickey Betts 12-bar blues, driven by Chuck Leavell's powerful pumping piano and Gregg's rumbling vocal. Betts takes a good solo to close an enjoyable-if-unoriginal song. A different take – without vocals – is included in the album's 2013 super-deluxe edition.

'Jessica' (Dickey Betts)

Released as a single (edited to 4:00), December 1973. Chart position: 65.
The follow-up to 'Ramblin' Man' was this toothsome instrumental, familiar to British TV viewers since 1977 as the opening theme to the long-running motoring programme *Top Gear*. The Allman's original version was used from 1977 to 1999.

The song is named after Dickey Bett's daughter Jessica, born on 14 May 1972. Betts recalled:

Here's the story which has been told many times. I had a general idea of a melody and a feeling for 'Jessica', but I couldn't get started on it; nothing was really adding up. My little girl Jessica – who at the time was an infant – crawled up to me and I started playing to her; playing to the feeling of the innocence of her personality. And soon, the whole song just fell together. The song was justly named after her for providing the needed inspiration.

'Jessica' displays the influence of legendary jazz guitarist Django Reinhardt. Betts said: 'Django only used two fingers to fret with, so I devised a melody that I could play with just the index and middle fingers'. Additionally, Betts' Nova Scotia ancestry includes the fiddle players of Prince Edward Sound. 'These fiddle players were known for possessing a very distinct style, and the style of the Prince Edward Sound fiddlers sounded just like the fiddle playing of my dad and my uncles. This provided me with an instinct for a melodic approach to playing'.

Another inspiration was perhaps unexpected: 18th-century German composer Johannes Brahms. Betts told *Music Aficionado* in 2016:

I don't know a damn thing about classical music, but I do love to listen to Brahms concertos for violin. I hear musical ideas in the music of Brahms, that I was using before I ever heard it in his music! I'm not bragging, I just get a big kick out of it. The first time that happened, I thought, 'Oh my god! He's stealing my licks!'. But what it really told me was that I was thinking in good solid musical terms. And it is very rewarding that, as a solid piece of music, 'Jessica' seems to have stood the test of time, and audiences are still glad to hear it when we play it today.

'Jessica' is just as well-regarded for Chuck Leavell's piano-playing as for the familiar guitar lick. Leavell: "Jessica' was the first song that gave me an opportunity to play and express myself as a musician. We knew we were going to need something very powerful on *Brothers And Sisters*. Fortunately, 'Jessica' was it, and I ended up with a nice spot on it'.

Fifty years later, 'Jessica' is still recognisable as a classic as soon as it begins. The seven minutes and 31 seconds fly past – such is the elegance of the Allman Brothers' most commercially-appealing instrumental work.

'Pony Boy' (Dickey Betts)

A pure country blues, which jumps and crackles. Betts sings and plays some exquisite dobro. 'A damn good tune', according to Gregg Allman. The song is structured in the style of Delta blues. Betts' reedy vocal doesn't quite live up to the gutbucket backing. Tommy Talton from the band Cowboy (who supported The Allman Brothers Band on tour in 1970/1971) sits in on acoustic guitar. At the end, you hear several members of the band playing the spoons on their knees: and why not?

Saturday, 28 July 1973, Watkins Glen, NY

In 1973, The Allman Brothers Band headlined the biggest concert *ever*: the Summer Jam at the Watkins Glen Grand Prix Raceway in New York, 250 miles northeast of New York City. The lineup was completed by Grateful Dead and The Band. Bunky Odom of ABB's management team said, 'We thought those three bands represented America. They were the three best American bands, and they related to each other, the music related, the fans related and they all knew each other. It was just a great fit'.

Each band was paid $117,500, and 150,000 tickets were sold for $10 each. The day before the festival, the bands planned to soundcheck. But – as with Woodstock four years before – thousands of fans without tickets decided to attend the event, abandoning their vehicles and blocking the roads around the raceway. The musicians were unable to drive to the site from their hotel in Horsesheads, New York: about 18 miles away. Helicopters were hired. An estimated 200,000 were already on site. Chuck Leavell: 'It was absolutely stunning, exhilarating and exciting to see this incredible mass of human beings. It was an ocean of bodies. We were all just really buzzed by the whole scene and situation'.

Roadie Joe Dan Petty told *Vintage Guitar* in 1996: 'I thought it was pretty well organized. There were over 700,000 people there, and I think about 90 per cent paid admission. Usually, such big concerts ended up becoming free festivals. It was amazing to stand onstage and look out at the audience. After about the first 10,000 people, the rest looked like wallpaper'.

'Watkins Glen was a special experience', says Dickey Betts. 'I had never seen that many people at once. It was looking at the Grand Canyon'.

'Watkins Glen was like three Woodstocks', wrote Gregg Allman.

Out of necessity, the soundchecks became public performances. Butch Trucks noted: 'That afternoon rehearsal ended up being my most powerful memory, because in daylight you could see 600,000 people stretched out in front of you – and my god, what a sight! Everyone should get up in front of 600,000 people sometime in their life. It's sort of intimidating but also very very inspiring'.

The following day, each of the bands performed long sets. 'We got the short stick on who would open and who would close', says the Grateful Dead's Bob Weir. 'As I recall, it was essentially determined by drawing cards out of a hat, because it was impossible to rank the bands. It would've been nice to have the lights, and we didn't get them because we played in daylight'.

The Grateful Dead were followed by The Band, who had not played together in a year. Their excellent two-hour set included several covers; some from their recently-recorded album *Moondog Matinee*. The 1995 CD *Live at Watkins Glen* purports to include a ten-song excerpt from The Band's set. However, only two of the tracks are from Watkins Glen. The original performances have been bootlegged, as has The Band's soundcheck.

For three hours, The Allman Brothers Band performed the following songs: 'Wasted Words', 'Done Somebody Wrong', 'Southbound', 'Stormy Monday', 'In Memory Of Elizabeth Reed', 'Come And Go Blues', 'Trouble No More', 'Blue

Sky', 'One Way Out', 'Statesboro Blues', 'Ramblin' Man', 'Jessica', 'Midnight Rider', 'You Don't Love Me', 'Les Brers In A Minor' and 'Whipping Post'. 'Come And Go Blues' was included on the 1976 live album *Wipe the Windows, Check the Oil, Dollar Gas*. A pretty decent recording of the whole show has been available on bootleg for years.

To close the night, members of all three bands jammed together – sloppily – on 'Not Fade Away', 'Reelin' And Rockin'', 'Let Me Wrap You In My Warm And Tender Love', 20 minutes of a one-chord 'Mountain Jam' (some of which was officially released in 2020), and, perhaps inevitably, 'Johnny B. Goode'. Butch Trucks told *Forbes* in 2016: 'After we finished playing, we all came out for the jam, and all I can say is it was an absolute disaster. It was a jam that couldn't possibly have worked because of the mixture of drugs. The Band was all drunk as skunks, the Dead was all tripping, and we were full of coke'.

Robert Santelli in *Aquarius Rising* in 1980:

Many historians claimed that the Watkins Glen event was the largest gathering of people in the history of the United States. In essence, that meant that on July 28, one out of every 350 people living in America at the time was listening to the sounds of rock at the New York state racetrack. Considering that most of those who attended the event hailed from the northeast, and that the average age of those present was approximately 17 to 24, close to one out of every three young people from Boston to New York was at the festival.

Five months after this landmark concert, the Allman Brothers played the Cow Palace in San Francisco on New Year's Eve, in a performance nationally broadcast on KSAN. Gregg Allman wrote forty years later: 'If that tour was as good as we ever played with that group of guys, then that show was our pinnacle'. Jerry Garcia and Bill Kreutzmann sat in for much of the second set and encore, with Kreutzmann taking over for Trucks, who was dosed with LSD and unable to continue playing. Boz Scaggs played organ. A 12-minute 'Jessica' feels succinct when followed by a 50-minute 'Les Brers In A Minor', which segues into 'Whipping Post', and then impromptu versions of Ray Sharpe's 'Linda Lou' and Ronnie Hawkins' 'Mary Lou'. This is followed by 30 minutes of 'Bo Diddley' interpolated with 'Mountain Jam', another 30 of an unknown song listed on bootlegs as 'Save My Life', and a lengthy encore of 'You Don't Love Me', 'Will The Circle Be Unbroken?' and a reprise of 'Mountain Jam'.

Then, on 4 June 1974, the group headlined the rain-soaked Georgia Jam at Fulton Stadium in Atlanta. The Allman Brothers were often lumped in with the 'southern rock' genre – never more obvious than the supporting line-up here, despite the varied musical menu: The Marshall Tucker Band, Lynyrd Skynyrd and Grinderswitch. No doubt the Allmans simply took their $150,000 pay cheque and didn't bat an eyelid.

Win, Lose or Draw (1975)

Personnel:
Gregg Allman: lead vocals, Hammond organ, clavinet, acoustic guitar
Richard Betts: lead, slide and acoustic guitar, lead vocals ('Just Another Love Song', 'Louisiana Lou And Three Card Monty John', 'Sweet Mama')
Jaimoe: drums, percussion
Chuck Leavell: piano, Fender Rhodes, Moog synthesizer, clavinet, background vocals
Butch Trucks: drums, congas, percussion, timpani
Lamar Williams: bass
Johnny Sandlin: acoustic guitar, drums, percussion
Bill Stewart: drums
Recorded February-July 1975 at Capricorn Sound, Macon, Georgia; The Record Plant, L.A. Producers: Johnny Sandlin, The Allman Brothers Band
Release date: August 1975
Chart position: 5

Following the huge success of *Brothers and Sisters*, Gregg Allman toured as a solo act in March and April 1974. The Gregg Allman Band included Jaimoe, Chuck Leavell and members of Cowboy. After the Allman Brothers' 23-date summer tour, the album *The Gregg Allman Tour* followed in October.

Dickey Betts released his debut solo album *Highway Call* in September 1974. This was recorded at Capricorn in Macon between band tour commitments. The album reached a respectable 19 in the charts. This activity inevitably slowed the band's momentum, and they played no concerts between August 1974 and August 1975.

The band's sixth album *Win, Lose or Draw* was also recorded at Capricorn, with sessions stretching across the first six months of 1975. Gregg Allman recorded his vocals in California, away from the rest of the band – producer Johnny Sandlin travelling from Macon to Los Angeles with the master tapes for the recording. Allman was about to formalise his highly-publicised relationship with Cher – they married in Las Vegas on 30 June 1975. Gregg writes:

I probably did spend too much time out in California. But at that point it was easy to run: those sessions were the worst experience I ever had in a studio. It wasn't just me though: they were bad for all of us. Where the earlier albums had come together pretty quickly, this recording stretched from February to July '75. Very rarely were all of us in the studio at the same time. The only three who regularly showed up, were Jaimoe, Chuck and Lamar. Even so, Jaimoe and Butch still missed playing drums on a couple of tracks – Sandlin and Bill Stewart had to play the drums instead. And then there was Dickey, who seemed like he only cared about playing on songs that he wrote, and tried to dictate the entire process.

Butch Trucks said in 2001: '*Win, Lose Or Draw* was a very dry, dull, boring piece of shit, because we spent eight months in the studio doing it'.

Chuck Leavell agrees: 'Those were tough times for the band. Maybe *Win, Lose Or Draw* didn't have the overall power of *Brothers and Sisters*, but there were some good things on it'.

The cracks were beginning to show. The album sounds frustrated, disjointed and tired. Nevertheless, the band's stock ensured another top-five album, which quickly went Gold.

'Can't Lose What You Never Had' (Muddy Waters)

By 1975, the Allmans were on the verge of collapse, and Gregg was increasingly alienated from his bandmates, and dependent on drugs to get through it all. That lost-soul murk, envelops this version of Muddy Waters' song from the Allmans' *Win, Lose or Draw* album. Gregg had never sounded so weary or burdened.
David Browne, *Rolling Stone*, 7 May 2017

The throbbing double-drum shuffle, funky clavinet and trademark rising guitar phrases mark out familiar territory on this radical re-working of the 1964 Muddy Waters song. Chuck Leavell adds some tasty piano, and Dickey's solo is wonderful. But Gregg's vocal is weary, and this drags down the entire song, despite the perky tempo and syncopated rhythm. The live version from *Wipe the Windows, Check the Oil, Dollar Gas* has much more fire.

A demo of this song, recorded in February 1975, is included on *One More Try: An Anthology* (1997).

'Just Another Love Song' (Dickey Betts)
Dangerously close to a carbon copy of 'Blue Sky', but without that song's charm, 'Just Another Love Song' is pure country and would perhaps have fit better on a Great Southern album. It's pleasant and unassuming but lacks any bite.

'Nevertheless' (Gregg Allman)
Released as a single, 1975. Chart position: 67
A lop-sided Jaimoe/Butch rhythm has acres of space in the verses. There's tinkling piano, and a punchy vocal from Gregg. Dickey plays some subtle slide, but the song doesn't maintain its energy, despite its brevity.

'Win, Lose Or Draw' (Gregg Allman)

'Win, Lose Or Draw' is the song that hits most people hardest on first hearing. It's an interior monologue movie of a man in jail and the changes he goes

through. 'Oh I'm so far away', Gregg sings with a clear and aching vocal (His voice here isn't as gravelly as usual, which also helps set the mood), and Betts responds with subtle and moving slide work. The picture is of a man locked up, watching his woman slip away, lost in futility ('Cold desperation I feel') in an anonymous cell with a stranger. Though not a blues in style or structure, it's sad and moving.
Tony Glover, *Rolling Stone*, 6 November 1975

One of the album highlights, the title track was written about Greg's friend Chank Middleton. It's a country waltz with delicate lead guitar and a strong vocal from Gregg.

An early acoustic demo recorded in September 1974 is included on *One More Try: An Anthology* (1997). Readers are directed to Eric Church's outstanding version on *All My Friends – Celebrating the Songs of Gregg Allman* (2014).

'Louisiana Lou And Three Card Monty John' (Dickey Betts)
Released as a single, 1975. Chart position: 78
Betts' limitations as a vocalist are evident in this driving story which has typically-fluid piano-playing from Chuck Leavell, and intertwined half-time double-drumming. The influence and bounce of Bob Dylan's 'Lily, Rosemary And The Jack Of Hearts' is very evident, along with the rustic feel of The Band. It's a decent song: especially the gorgeous guitar solo in the last 30 seconds.

'High Falls' (Dickey Betts)
The best song on the album by some measure, at 14 minutes, this magnificent swinging jazz instrumental is the longest Allman Brothers Band studio track. It's named after a Georgia state park near Macon.

It starts with a slow 90-second build – not unlike 'Les Brers In A Minor' – pulsing and shimmering. The outstanding Butch/Jaimoe/Lamar rhythm section sets the pace with closely interlinked drums and bass, leaving lots of room for Dickey's soft guitar leads and Chuck's muted electric piano. It sounds a lot like Sea Level's first album: this is a very good thing.

Chuck Leavell said, 'I play Fender Rhodes on that piece. I thought it was a beautiful song, and I do think that 'High Falls' is largely overlooked'. He's right.

'Sweet Mama' (Billy Joe Shaver)
This is a plodding blues boogie sung by Dickey Betts and written by his pal, the Texan country singer Billy Joe Shaver. Other than old blues songs, it's the only song the band recorded in their first spell together that they did not write themselves.

Bob Dylan mentions Shaver in the song 'I Feel A Change Comin' On' on the album *Together Through Life* (2009): 'I'm listening to Billy Joe Shaver, and I'm reading James Joyce'.

Wipe the Windows, Check the Oil, Dollar Gas (1976)

Personnel:
Gregg Allman: lead vocals, organ, clavinet, guitar
Richard Betts: lead vocals, lead and slide guitar
Jaimoe: drums, percussion
Chuck Leavell: piano, electric piano, background vocals
Butch Trucks: drums, percussion, timpani
Lamar Williams: bass
Recorded 1973-1975
Producers: The Allman Brothers Band
Release date: November 1976
Chart position: 75

Despite the release of *Win, Lose or Draw* and two minor hit singles in 1975, Capricorn cashed in on their biggest asset with the double compilation, *The Road Goes On Forever*, at the end of that year. The impeccable track list was 'Black Hearted Woman', 'Dreams', 'Whipping Post', 'Midnight Rider', 'Statesboro Blues', 'Stormy Monday', 'Hoochie Coochie Man', 'Stand Back', 'One Way Out', 'Blue Sky', 'Hot 'Lanta', 'Ain't Wastin' Time No More', 'Melissa', 'Wasted Words', 'Jessica', 'Ramblin' Man' and 'Little Martha'. A 2001 re-release adds 13 more songs, with tracks from later in the 1970s, including the live album, *Wipe the Windows, Check the Oil, Dollar Gas*, released at the end of 1976.

The Allman Brothers Band's last gig before splitting up was on 4 May 1976 at the Civic Center in Roanoke, Virginia. Gregg wrote, 'The truth was we couldn't fucking stand each other'. The breaking point was his decision to testify against his tour manager – security man and delivery guy (i.e., drug supplier) Scooter Herring – at a trial in June 1976. Gregg:

> There was a lot of confusion about what was going on and what Scooter had done, but it didn't take long to figure things out. Scooter was being arrested because he'd been helping me buy drugs, but they nabbed him not because he was buying, but because they said he was selling. I did everything I could to avoid testifying, but it was made clear to me that my back was against the wall; there was no way to dodge a federal prosecutor. I got that horrible sinking-type feeling, like a good friend had died or something. Eventually, I was granted immunity from prosecution in exchange for my testimony in front of the grand jury and later at the trial. Fuck me, man, I didn't have no choice.

Allman did have a choice: to invoke the Fifth Amendment. Herring was convicted on five counts of conspiracy to distribute cocaine and received a 75-year prison sentence. This was later reduced, and he was subsequently pardoned by President Jimmy Carter. Presumably, coincidentally, The Allman Brothers Band had headlined a benefit for Carter – then Governor of Georgia – in November 1975.

Above: The Gray House at 2844 Riverside Avenue, Jacksonville, the location for the Allman Brothers Band's first jam session on 23 March 1969. (*Courtesy Bob Beatty, atfillmoreeastbook.com*)

Right: The original Allman Brothers Band in Macon, Georgia, April 1969. (*Courtesy of the Lyndon Family/Big House Museum Archives*)

Left: The monumental debut album recorded in New York City in August 1969. *(Capricon / Universal Music Group)*

Right: Outside t 315 College St. in Macon, Georgia, April 1969. *(Courtesy of the Lyndon Family/Big House Museum Archives)*

Left: Dickey and Berry in Piedmont Park, Atlanta, 1969. *(Courtesy of the Lyndon Family/Big House Museum Archives)*

Right: The second album, *Idlewild South*. The album's title comes from the band's nickname for a rustic cabin they used for rehearsals. (*Capricon / Universal Music Group*)

Left: Duane in Piedmont Park, Atlanta, 1969. (*Courtesy of the Lyndon Family/Big House Museum Archives*)

Right: *At Fillmore East*. 'The truest fulfilment of Duane Allman's musical vision' and one of the greatest live albums of all time. (*Capricon / Universal Music Group*)

Left: Road case at the Big House Museum. (*Courtesy Bob Beatty, atfillmoreeastbook.com*)

Right: Jaimoe and Berry in the studio. (*Courtesy of the Lyndon Family/ Big House Museum Archives*)

Right: *Eat A Peach* (1972). The band's first top ten album. Gregg Allman said, 'We'd been through hell, but somehow we were rolling bigger than ever'. (*Capricon / Universal Music Group*)

Left: Jaimoe and Butch recording *Eat A Peach* at Criteria Studios, Miami. (*Courtesy of the Lyndon Family/Big House Museum Archives*)

Right: The short-lived five-piece lineup in 1972. (*Courtesy of the Lyndon Family/Big House Museum Archives*)

Left: *Brothers and Sisters* (1973) sold over 1,000,000 copies within a month of release and spent five weeks at the top of the *Billboard* album charts. (*Capricon / Universal Music Group*)

Right: The 1973-1976 line-up with Chuck Leavell and Lamar Williams. (*Courtesy of the Lyndon Family/ Big House Museum Archives*)

Above: *Win, Lose Or Draw* (1975). The band's sixth album. The cracks were beginning to show. (*Capricon / Universal Music Group*)

Right: *Wipe the Windows, Check the Oil, Dollar Gas.* A live album released after the band had split up in 1976. It's beautifully recorded and brilliantly performed. (*Capricon / Universal Music Group*)

Left: *Enlightened Rogues* (1979). The first and the best of the three albums from the band's first reunion. (*Capricon / Universal Music Group*)

Right: *Reach for the Sky* (1980). Not their finest work. (*Arista / Sony Music Entertainment*)

Left: Dangerous Dan, Jaimoe and Dickey. May, 1979, in Wheeling, WV. (*Courtesy Art Dobie*)

Dickey Betts, May 1979 in Wheeling, WV. (*Courtesy Art Dobie*)

Right: *Brothers of the Road* (1981). Professionally written and recorded and cleanly produced but displaying an air of desperation. (*Arista / Sony Music Entertainment*)

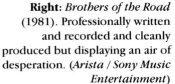

Left: *The Dream* box set (1989). Four CDs, six albums, five hours, 55 songs. (*Polydor / UMC*)

Right: *Seven Turns* (1990). There was a lot riding on the Allman Brothers' first album in nine years. (*Epic / Sony Music Entertainment*)

Left: *Shades of Two Worlds* (1991). Warren Haynes was now firmly at the helm. (*Epic / Sony Music Entertainment*)

Right: *An Evening With The Allman Brothers Band First Set* (1992). The first of two live albums from the 1990s-era band. The playing is nothing short of magnificent. (*Epic / Sony Music Entertainment*)

Left: *Where It All Begins* (1994) - The band's last studio album with Dickey Betts. (*Epic / Sony Music Entertainment*)

Right: *An Evening With The Allman Brothers Band Second Set* (1995). A terrific live album which combines some well-chosen classics with four tracks from *Where It All Begins* and a cover of a Willie Dixon song. (*Epic / Sony Music Entertainment*)

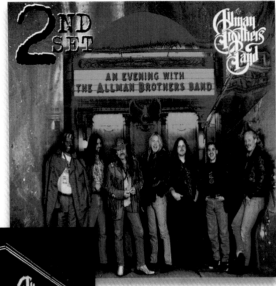

Left: *Peakin' At The Beacon* (2000). Enter Derek Trucks, farewell Dickey Betts. (*Epic / Sony Music Entertainment*)

Right: *Hittin' The Note* (2003) The band's strongest and most consistent studio release since *Idlewild South*. (*Sanctuary / Peach*)

Left: Derek Trucks, August 2005. (*Courtesy Gary Nagle*)

Right and below: Founder members Gregg Allman and Jaimoe at the band's final show in October 2014. (*Courtesy Gary Nagle*)

Right and below: Otiel Burbridge and Warren Haynes at the band's final show, October 2014. (*Courtesy Gary Nagle*)

Right: The road goes on forever. The Allman Brothers Band's last ever concert in October 2014. (*Courtesy Gary Nagle*)

Left: Duane and Berry's memorials in Macon. (*Courtesy Bob Beatty, atfillmoreeastbook.com*)

Right: Little Martha's memorial in Macon. (*Courtesy Bob Beatty, atfillmoreeastbook.com*)

Left: Elizabeth Reed's grave in Macon. (*Courtesy Bob Beatty, atfillmoreeastbook.com*)

Right and below: The Big House Museum, Macon, which opened in 2007. (*Courtesy John Lynskey*)

Left: *One Way Out: Live at the Beacon Theatre* (2004) showcases the energy and control of the rejuvenated band, as recorded during their 2003 residency in New York. (*Sanctuary / Peach*)

Right: *Trouble No More* (2020). A five-CD career retrospective. All of the band's 13 line-ups are represented. (*Mercury / UMG*)

Left: *The Fox Box* (2004). Three complete concerts recorded at Atlanta's Fox Theatre: 24-26 September 2004. The Allman Brothers played 50 different songs across these three shows. (*Peach*)

THE FOX BOX

9/24/04   9/25/04   9/26/04
THE FOX THEATRE • ATLANTA, GEORGIA

Right: *The Beacon Box* (2009). This hefty 47-disc set contains every gig performed in the band's spring 2009 residency at the Beacon in New York. (*Peach*)

The band refused to communicate with Allman after the incident. They'd been working on another album, but any completed recordings remain unheard. Gregg wrote:

The band officially broke up when Jaimoe wrote a letter to the Macon newspaper, which stated that there was no more Allman Brothers Band. Not long after, Butch and Dickey came out individually and said the same thing, with Dickey doing it in Rolling Stone. I remember in that issue, there was a picture of Betts and a quote from him saying, 'I'll never play onstage with Gregg Allman again'. No problem, brother! I just wish we had held him to that. Truth is, there ain't one thing or person alone that broke up the Allman Brothers. It was everything and everyone – Scooter, my recording Laid Back, my living in L.A., the drugs. They were all just easy excuses; ways of talking around the unavoidable truth: that none of us knew when or how to walk away.

Allman and Betts continued their solo careers. Allman founded The Gregg Allman Band and worked with his third wife Cher. Betts formed Great Southern in 1978, releasing two albums, but playing 500-seat bars. Trucks formed his own jazz rock group and lectured at Florida State University. Meanwhile, Jaimoe, Leavell and Williams – who'd performed as We Three in support of The Allman Brothers Band – regrouped as the jazz-fusion collective Sea Level with guitarist Jimmy Nalls. They recorded several excellent albums between 1977 and 1981.
Chuck Leavell recalls:

The three of us would always go down to the soundcheck early and we would just play. The birth of Sea Level was in September 1975. (The Allman Brothers) were playing in New Haven, and Gregg and Dickey were really late for the gig. The crowd was getting restless. We agreed to go on. We probably played for 30 minutes, and it seemed to help the situation.

Jaimoe suggests: 'Just listen closely to *Wipe the Windows, Check the Oil, Dollar Gas* and you'll hear the rhythm section of Chuck, Lamar and myself. We were there to play, man, and you can hear the shifting of the way the music was sounding.'
Wipe the Windows, Check the Oil, Dollar Gas is a very good live album, highlighting the best of the post-Duane period. Whilst not in the league of *At Fillmore East* (but what is?), it's beautifully recorded, brilliantly performed, and has a warm production showing the strength of the band at their commercial peak: especially the consistently tremendous musicianship of Chuck Leavell and Lamar Williams. Only one song is repeated from *At Fillmore East*: a spiritual 17-minute version of 'In Memory Of Elizabeth Reed'. This album is certainly worthy of your attention.

Side One: :
1. Introduction/'Wasted Words', 2. 'Southbound', 3. 'Ramblin' Man' (26 September 1973, Winterland, San Francisco)

Side Two:
1. 'In Memory Of Elizabeth Reed' (26 September 1973, Winterland, San Francisco)

Side Three:
1. 'Ain't Wastin' Time No More' (31 December 1972, The Warehouse, New Orleans), 2. 'Come And Go Blues' (28 July 1973, The Summer Jam, Watkins Glen, New York), 3. 'Can't Lose What You Never Had' (22 October 1975, Civic Auditorium, Bakersfield)

Side Four:
1.'Don't Want You No More' (22 October 1975, Civic Auditorium, Bakersfield), 2. 'It's Not My Cross To Bear' (22 October 1975, Civic Auditorium, Bakersfield), 3. 'Jessica' (24 October 1975, Oakland Coliseum)

The 2005 archive release *Nassau Coliseum, Uniondale, NY: 5/1/73* documents a full 1973 show. The complete Winterland concert of 26 September 1973 was made available as part of the 2013 super deluxe edition of *Brothers And Sisters*. I should also mention live versions of 'Statesboro Blues' and 'One Way Out' recorded at the same venue on 13 March 1976, which are available on the 1997 album *Alive Down South*. The whole show was broadcast live on WLIR.

Part II: 16 August 1978-23 January 1982

Wednesday, 16 August 1978, New York City, NY

Between 1977 and 1982, the Dr. Pepper Summer Music Festival presented a diverse programme of artists in Central Park, New York. Ten weeks of concerts at Wollman Rink between July and September 1978, included Frankie Valli, Al Di Meola, UK, Atlanta Rhythm Section, Pablo Cruise, Arlo Guthrie, Emmylou Harris, David Crosby and Stephen Stills, Laura Nyro, Richie Havens, The Patti Smith Group, Southside Johnny and the Asbury Jukes, The Kinks, Muddy Waters, Robert Palmer, Meat Loaf, Chicago and many others. Nestled in this varied schedule – on 16 August 1978 – The Dickey Betts Band introduced some special guests for a five-song set: Gregg Allman, Butch Trucks and Jaimoe. Gregg recalled:

One day I was taking a shower at my mother's house. I got the towel wrapped around me and I walked out into the living room, and there sits Dickey Betts. He had actually rented a prop plane from his home in Sarasota, to fly over to Daytona. He told me, 'I wanted to come down here and talk to you about reforming the band'. I just said, 'Oh', and the words hung there for a minute. It was decided that Butch, Jaimoe and I would join Dickey's band for a few songs at their concert in Central Park. They brought us up one by one, and I was the last one to be called. When we walked out there, the place went apeshit.

The large crowd was treated to renditions of 'One Way Out', 'You Don't Love Me', 'Stormy Monday', 'Statesboro Blues' and 'Blue Sky'. Greg told *People* early in 1979: 'It had been a while since I'd heard a crowd like that. It scared the hell out of me. But that clinched it to go on'.

The reunion had been brewing for some time. Gregg and Dickey had met by chance at Jimmy Carter's inauguration in January 1977. Towards the end of the year, Gregg attended sessions for Betts' *Atlanta's Burning Down* in Miami to discuss a possible reunion. Phil Walden was in attendance and soon started planning, starting with Butch Trucks.

Trucks told *Rolling Stone* in 1979:

Phil called me. I said, 'No, no way'. I had my own band and I just wasn't interested. Then one day I was playing in Tampa with my band, and I ran into Dickey. We sat up all night and talked and he played some new tunes for me, including 'Crazy Love', and I started getting excited. I saw how together Dickey was. I'd finally got over a bad drinking problem I had, and he said Gregg seemed to be in excellent shape. So we started talking seriously about putting it back together at that point.

Despite complex internal politics and the complications of heavy drug use, Allman, Betts, Trucks and Jaimoe agreed to regroup. Initial rehearsals included

Chuck Leavell and Lamar Williams, and eight days after the Central Park gig, the 1973-1976 lineup performed at Capricorn's annual barbeque.

However, Leavell and Williams remained committed to Sea Level (Jaimoe had left earlier in the year, and was a free agent). To complete this new iteration of The Allman Brothers Band, 'Dangerous' Dan Toler and David Goldflies moved across from Great Southern. Toler – a genuinely-talented player – had worked in several groups with his brother David (primarily Melting Pot between 1969 and 1976), signed to Capricorn. Bassist Goldflies had played in groups around Cincinnati prior to joining Great Southern. Both had been on stage at Central Park.

By the end of 1978, the band had returned to Criteria in Miami to record a new album with Tom Dowd.

It wasn't as momentous as if, say, Lennon and McCartney announced their reunion, but the rapprochement in Miami was perhaps even more unlikely. Nearly three years after their acrimonious breakup, Allman, Betts and the remnants of the original Allman Brothers Band cautiously gathered in a studio to piece together what had been one the premiere acts of the mid-1970s. Gregg told *People* in February 1979: 'We feel like it's the first time together. We're fresh. We've all come through a lot, and learned a lot from it'.

Enlightened Rogues (1979)

Personnel:
Gregg Allman: organ, Fender Rhodes, clavinet, lead vocals ('Can't Take It With You',
'Need Your Love So Bad', 'Blind Love', 'Try It One More Time', 'Just Ain't Easy'),
backing vocals
Dickey Betts: electric, acoustic and slide guitar, lead vocals ('Crazy Love', 'Try It
One More Time', 'Sail Away')
David Goldflies: bass
Jaimoe: drums, congas
Dan Toler: electric and acoustic guitar
Butch Trucks: drums, congas, backing vocals
Joe Lala: percussion ('Pegasus', 'Blind Love', 'Try It One More Time')
Bonnie Bramlett: background vocals ('Crazy Love')
Jim Essery: harmonica ('Can't Take It With You', 'Need Your Love So Bad', 'Blind
Love', 'Just Ain't Easy'
John Lundahl: guitar ('Can't Take It With You')
Mimi Hart: background vocals ('Sail Away')
Recorded December 1978 January 1979 at Criteria, Miami, Florida
Producer: Tom Dowd
Release date: March 1979
Chart position: 9

And so, The Allman Brothers Band returned to Criteria with Tom Dowd to try
to recreate past glories. In parts, they succeeded. Dowd: 'We tried very hard to
reach the classic sound. We worked our fingers to the bone, but it was laborious'.
   The band were upbeat about their new album. Gregg told *Rolling Stone* in
May 1979:

> This album came off better than any we've ever done before. I think we really
> did it like a bunch of pros, man. We took six weeks and rehearsed it at the
> warehouse, took a little bit of time off, then went in there and slam-bang got
> it done. We knew what we were doing, plus we were working with Tommy
> Dowd: who's the best, in my book. I enjoyed cutting this album more than
> anyone I ever cut, except *At Fillmore East*. Between Tom producing and all of
> us playing together, everything went pretty smoothly. The only thing I didn't
> like about recording that album was David Goldflies the new bass player. The
> guy must've thought he was getting paid by the note, the way he would play
> those banjo notes on the bass. Despite all that, *Enlightened Rogues* was a good
> record, and I liked it a lot.

The album was strong and sold well, going Platinum within two weeks of
release, and entering the *Billboard* top 10. Betts' 'Pegasus' garnered the band
their first Grammy nomination – for Best Rock Instrumental Performance:
losing to 'Rockestra Theme' by Wings.

Chuck Leavell commented at the time: 'It sounds good, but it sounds real familiar. I was kind of hoping they'd go a little bit further out and experiment with a little more contemporary things. I thought originally that people would get turned off by that same old thing, but well, hell, man, that's what they liked about it'.

Gregg responded: 'People are always gonna have those opinions. I don't care what you put out, somebody's gonna have something bad to say about it. Those people ought to come see it live'.

John Swenson in *Rolling Stone*, practically gushed:

Enlightened Rogues takes its place not beside the empty, last-gasp *Win, Lose or Draw*, or even the slick and calculated *Brothers and Sisters*, but ranks with the group's greatest albums. Of course, the current twin-guitar sound falls short of the rich contrast between Duane Allman's fat, explosive tone and Dickey Betts' sweet, incisive harmony work on the earlier LPs, and Gregg Allman's once-terrifying singing has been humbled by tragedy. But whatever *Enlightened Rogues* lacks in virtuosity, it makes up for in emotional intensity.

The Village Voice's Robert Christgau wasn't convinced: 'Ronnie Van Zant himself couldn't breathe life into these songs, most of which Dickey Betts was saving up for the third Great Southern album: now never to be heard, which is one good thing'.

With the album finished in the early weeks of 1979, and a 60-date tour booked to begin in April, the band duly rehearsed in Dickey's home town of Saratoga, Florida, ahead of their first scheduled concert date for almost three years: at Pensacola Municipal Auditorium. After a support set from labelmates Wet Willie, this fourth iteration of The Allman Brothers Band opened with 'Don't Want You No More' and 'It's Not My Cross to Bear'. Their first set included four songs from *Enlightened Rogues*, along with 'Blue Sky' and 'In Memory Of Elizabeth Reed'. A powerful second set included 'Statesboro Blues', 'One Way Out', 'Southbound', 'Jessica', 'Whipping Post', and 'Try It One More Time' from *Enlightened Rogues.* The new track 'Pegasus' and 'Ramblin' Man' comprised a Betts-centric encore.

Meanwhile, in Jacksonville, Florida on 8 June 1979, Butch Trucks' sister-in-law Debbie gave birth to a boy. Debbie and her husband Chris named the boy Derek, after Eric Clapton's band Derek and the Dominos. More of Derek Trucks in due course.

'Crazy Love' (Dickey Betts)
Released as a single, March 1979. Chart position: 29
A beefy, commercial rocker written and sung by Dickey Betts, who also plays dirty slide guitar. There's nothing new here, but perhaps that's the point. 'Crazy Love' reached 29 in *Billboard*: their second and last top-30 hit.

The band's old friend Bonnie Bramlett sings typically strident background vocals, and also toured with them in this period, though she was never a formal member of the band.

'Can't Take It With You' (Dickey Betts, Don Johnson)

Released as a single, June 1979. Chart position: 105

Gregg sings a powerful boogie. The song's co-writers Betts and actor Don Johnson had become friends when Johnson was filming the movie *Return To Macon County Line* in 1976. The pair had previously written 'Bougainvillea' on *Dickey Betts & Great Southern*.

The trademark Allman Brothers signature ingredients are all in place here – the syncopated drums, throbbing organ, tough rasping vocals and harmony guitars. The track's closing minutes of loud and intense guitar accents are one of the album's highlights.

The song had real punch when played live in 1979 but sounded flaccid in 1980 and 1981.

Guitarist John Lundahl is credited with 'backup guitar' on this track. Extensive research has failed to find any information about Lundahl and his association with the band.

'Pegasus' (Dickey Betts)

'Pegasus' offers nothing new but is a pleasing, technically-accomplished and upbeat seven-minute instrumental with harmony guitars and tight band interplay: especially the short Trucks/Jaimoe drum break from 4:52 to 5:45. *Rolling Stone*'s John Swenson:

'Pegasus' ... compares favourably with 'In Memory Of Elizabeth Reed' and 'Blue Sky'. The group sweeps effortlessly through the tune's eight-part evolution. After the theme and first guitar solo, Allman displays the finest organ-playing of his career. At the end of his solo, the organ fills out the progression with a warm resolution that recalls Steve Winwood's magnificent music on Traffic's John Barleycorn Must Die. Betts enters for his solo, and the drummers move freely into orbit until the guitars and organ state the bridge in unison before the theme is again evoked, releasing the tension. Then the coda extends in enveloping filigrees, recapitulating the melodic ideas in a jazz-influenced approach reminiscent of the days when Duane Allman and Dickey Betts would stretch out an ending far beyond its possibilities: searching for that last ringing resolution; that perfect final note.

'Pegasus' would often extend to 30 minutes or more in concert performances.

'Need Your Love So Bad' (John Mertis)

The first song cut at these sessions is a perfectly presentable slab of 12/8 blues – the kind of music that musicians of this calibre can play in their sleep. Dan

Toler's solo is serviceable, if without much character. The song – probably most associated with Fleetwood Mac – was an occasional band favourite, performed regularly from 1979-1981 and into the 1990s.

'Blind Love' (B.B. King, Jules Taub)
This B.B. King song was first released in 1957, and the Allman Brothers cover is a rather obvious revision of the band's arrangement of 'Statesboro Blues'. As with the album's other tracks, it's entertaining and enjoyable, even when bordering on cliché. In May 1979, Dickey Betts told *Rolling Stone* of his guitar influences:

> I listened to Coltrane and Pharoah Sanders and all those people, but I think what you're talking about, the lyricism … I like Brahms. You know, the things he wrote for violin? The violin can really float a melody, and I try to do that with the guitar. Believe it or not, Brahms even does a lot of the climb-ups, like in 'Blind Love' on the new album, where the two guitars have the melody and it climbs right up – it's almost a signature of The Allman Brothers Band. … Well, Brahms does that same thing in a lot of his pieces, in a more sophisticated way, of course.

'Try It One More Time' (Dickey Betts, David Goldflies)
This is one of the album's better songs, even when it echoes 'Stand Back' from time to time. It opens with delicate Latin accents courtesy of percussionist Joe Lala. There's also a funky clavinet. Jaimoe and Trucks push their cross-rhythms through the whole song, and Dan Toler takes a tight guitar solo.

'Just Ain't Easy' (Gregg Allman)
Gregg's only song on the album is beautiful and brilliantly sung. It's a lost gem in the ABB catalogue, and one of their absolute best songs.

Since moving to Los Angeles in 1975, Gregg had become more famous for his celebrity lifestyle than his music. Those painful few years are laid out with candour – this isn't his usual *bad woman* song, but a heavy dose of morning-after despair.

> You want so bad to leave this whirlwind storm
> But you can't find no place to grab on
> So 'round and 'round you go again, and it just ain't easy

John Swenson: 'The references to his life in Los Angeles – his private and public hell – are right up front. The forceful image of a sleepwalker trapped in a recurrent dream has mythical resonance from Sisyphus to Bob Dylan's 'Memphis Blues Again', but Gregg Allman amplifies his terror through the knowledge of why he stays: 'Cause midnight's calling'. Allman's warning at song's end – sung over and over as the languid guitar lines spin out the punctuation – rings with the power of someone who's come to terms with his own disgrace: 'When you leave there, you got your hat down on your face".

Gregg wrote: 'That song is about Hollywood and how bad I wanted out of that place. It's about defeat and resignation, being on the bottom, and I think it turned out pretty good'.

Gregg's singing is magnificent, and Dickey's solos are sublime. An alternative version is included in the *Dreams* box set.

'Sail Away' (Dickey Betts)

A good Betts' original that's let down by the composer's indifferent skills as a singer – this song screams for Gregg's rich vocal tone. 'Sail Away' has a regretful mood; it sounds like a valediction:

Sail on, sail away
May all your dreams come true one day
Sail on, sail away
I wonder why I ever thought you'd stay

The gorgeous backing vocals are by Ohio-based folk singer Mimi Hart. Betts had seen her perform in a small venue in Columbus, and offered her a job singing backup with the band, but she declined to join full-time. Mimi said, 'Going into the studio with The Allman Brothers was a great experience, especially because they recorded with Tom Dowd. We recorded in Miami, and it wasn't astonishing so much because I sang a lot – because I didn't – but because I learned and listened'.

Reach for the Sky (1980)

Personnel:
Gregg Allman: keyboards, lead vocals ('Mystery Woman', 'Angeline', 'Keep On Keeping On', 'So Long')
Dickey Betts: guitar, lead vocals ('Hell & High Water', 'I Got A Right To Be Wrong', 'Famous Last Words'
David Goldflies: bass
Jaimoe: drums
Dan Toler: guitar
Butch Trucks: drums, percussion
Recorded May 1980 at Pyramid Eye Recording Studio, Lookout Mountain, Georgia
Producers: Mike Lawler, Johnny Cobb
Release date: August 1980
Chart position: 27

Capricorn Records – who'd released all of the band's albums to this point – was sold to PolyGram Records in late 1979. The band signed a new deal with Arista, brokered by the label's founder and president Clive Davis.

Flush from the multiplatinum releases of Barry Manilow, Davis had signed Grateful Dead and The Kinks in 1976, and took on Dionne Warwick and Aretha Franklin in 1979/1980. The Allman Brothers don't merit a mention in his otherwise exhaustive autobiography.

Reach For The Sky and its follow-up *Brothers Of The Road* are the band's low point.

Gregg:

We did two insipid albums on Arista – *Reach for the Sky* and *Brothers of the Road* – and you won't find a copy in this house, and I doubt that any of the other guys have those records either. It was like a whole different band made those records. We had background singers, songwriters, synthesizers – fuck me, man. Those two awful albums for Arista were the price I had to pay for that drinking, and, unfortunately, all our fans had to pay that price too. But the real crime was how I lost sight of the music.

Reach For The Sky was recorded at Pyramid Eye studio in Lookout Mountain on the Tennessee/Georgia border: about two hours south of Nashville. The studio had built in 1976, and was owned by Scott Maclellan: heir to the Provident Life Insurance Company. Ten years before, he'd played in a local Chattanooga band called Humor, who'd supported the Allmans in 1971. The studio had been used by Melissa Manchester, Cowboy and Wet Willie. According to a *Billboard* article dated 1 November 1980, 'Dickey Betts' solo album was recorded there' (presumably 1978's *Atlanta's Burning Down*). Another client was the duo Lawler and Cobb, who recorded their only album *Men From Nowhere* at Pyramid Eye at the beginning of 1980. Mike Lawler and Johnny Cobb were hired to produce *Reach For The Sky*. Sessions took place in May 1980, with overdubs completed at LSI Studios and Young 'Un Sound, both in Nashville. The album was mixed at Axis Sound in Atlanta.

The back cover photograph shows the band on Sunset Rock on Lookout Mountain's western edge. Once sessions were completed, Mike Lawler joined The Allman Brothers Band.

Rolling Stone reviewed the album in 1980:

The current sound is thicker and heavier, close to funk in spots. Rather than sounding just plain stoned and out of it (the way he did last year), Gregg Allman at least has the aggrieved tone of the town drunk wrangling with a cop. But – if possible – everything is even less convincing. Practically all the cuts trade shamelessly on an image the Allmans stopped living out years ago. Once again, the only Allman in The Allman Brothers Band is pretty near irrelevant. Dickey Betts is the dominant personality here, and he has the charisma and poetry of a parking meter. The irony of a technician like Betts taking over, is that the whole group seems to have gotten slovenly as craftsmen. The players try a bit of everything to keep the music moving, yet they can't make up for *Reach for the Sky's* emotional hollowness.
Tom Carson, *Rolling Stone*, 16 October 1980

'Hell & High Water' (Dickey Betts)
The album opens with pure gospel, before morphing into an uneasy mix of gospel-country blues and disco. Gregg is fully committed at least, and the band work though some tricky changes, but the end result is a long way from classic Allman Brothers Band.

'Mystery Woman' (Gregg Allman, Dan Toler)
Released as a single, 1981. Did not chart.
Here, the band attempt and fail to be The Doobie Brothers... the guitars and rhythm section have a lighter, more commercial touch. It sounds pleasant enough until the first instrumental break, which sounds like it's been patched in from another song entirely.

'From The Madness Of The West' (Dickey Betts)
The best track on the album by far, 'From The Madness Of The West' is 'High Falls' part two; a jazz-tinged but drivingly-powerful Dickey Betts instrumental full of technique and skill – especially the always-impressive rhythm section.

'I Got A Right To Be Wrong' (Dickey Betts)
This standard blues boogie strays perilously close to Lynyrd Skynyrd territory – perhaps Dickey had been listening to Street Survivors' 'You Got That Right', which this song closely resembles in tempo, tone and title.

'Angeline' (Dickey Betts, Johnny Cobb, Mike Lawler)
Released as a single, 1980. Chart position: 58
Another commercial song, sung by Gregg, with some nice piano work and a fluent guitar solo. It was the album's lead single, so presumably, it was goodwill alone that propelled it into the lower reaches of the UK singles chart in spring 1980.

'Famous Last Words' (Dickey Betts, Bonnie Bramlett)
A forgettable rocker, with Dickey singing in a high register: which ill-suits both him and the song. A clavinet burbles away. Betts' vocal is mixed low and supported by backing vocals.

'Keep On Keepin' On' (Dickey Betts, Dan Toler)
More hints of funk, as Gregg pushes his vocals too far, belting out the trite lyric, viz., 'I don't care what everybody's gotta say / I'm gonna love you anyway / Even if you don't care any longer / My little bit of love keeps getting stronger'.

'So Long' (Gregg Allman, Dan Toler)
The album closes with the wonderful, mellow, valedictory 'So Long'. There's a sadness to the song, with it's plaintive harmonica and groaning vocals. It builds to an excellent long guitar solo, presumably from Dan Toler which flows and ebbs beautifully.

Brothers of the Road (1981)

Personnel:
Gregg Allman: organ, acoustic guitar, lead vocals ('Leavin'', 'Straight From The Heart', 'Maybe We Can Go Back To Yesterday', 'Never Knew How Much (I Needed You)', 'Things You Used To Do', 'I Beg Of You')
Dickey Betts: lead, slide, and acoustic guitar, lead vocals ('Brothers Of The Road', 'The Heat Is On', 'The Judgment', 'Two Rights')
David 'Rook' Goldflies: bass
Mike Lawler: piano, synthesizer, clavinet
'Dangerous' Dan Toler: lead and rhythm guitar
David 'Frankie' Toler: drums
Butch Trucks: drums
Charlie Daniels: fiddle ('Brothers Of The Road')
Jimmy Hall: sax ('Never Knew How Much (I Needed You)'
Mark 'Tito' Morris: percussion
Thomas Cain, Johnny Cobb, Jimmy Hall, Chip Young, Greg Guidry, Joy Lannon, Donna McElroy, Keith England, Jeff Silverman, Randall Hart, Peter Kingsberry, Joe Pizzulo: backing vocals
Recorded March 1981 at Young'un Sound, Nashville, Tennessee
Producer: John Ryan
Release date: August 1981
Chart position: 44

Founder member Jaimoe left the band in November 1980. By all accounts, Dickey Betts fired him for asking too closely about the band's finances. Jaimoe – a crucial cornerstone of the band's unique sound – was replaced by David 'Frankie' Toler: Dan Toler's twin brother and another alumnus of Great Southern.

Returning to the studio in March 1981 to record their second album for Arista – *Brothers of the Road* – label head-honcho Clive Davis recruited producer John Ryan. Ryan had co-produced three albums for arena-rockers Styx between 1972 and 1974, and had just scored a top-10 hit with Pure Prairie League's 'Let Me Love You Tonight'. Davis was looking for a smoother AOR sound for ABB, and perhaps a hit single. They were rewarded with both. Gregg: 'Arista wanted us to go into this whole pop-culture Michael Jackson-type thing, and we weren't buying that. We're the Allman Brothers, not the damn Osmond Brothers!'.

Ryan took the band back to Young'un Sound at 114 17th Avenue South, Nashville, where some overdubs for *Reach For The Sky* had been completed. After the sessions, the band again set out on tour, adding backing vocalists Bonnie Gallie and Keith England alongside Mike Lawler's banks of keyboards.
Keith England:

My family's move to Sarasota, Florida in my late teens would lead me to a close friendship, songwriting and singing with Gregg Allman. This culminated in writing, recording and subsequent touring with later versions of The Allman Brothers Band as a background singer, occasionally stepping out front-stage-centre to sing lead on those nights when head colds or throat infections rendered the lead singers in the band unable to answer the bell. For such brilliant artists as Gregg Allman and Dickey Betts to trust me with their songs in front of thousands of people, was truly an honour and a thrill which I'll never forget. I went from playing to 20 or 30 people in a nightclub, to a football stadium full of people overnight... and back again almost as quickly. Such is life.

Reading between the lines, it appears Allman and Betts couldn't be bothered singing their own songs any more. Video footage of the concert at the Capital Theatre in December 1981 shows them going through the motions, though England stays firmly at the back. Mike Lawler was allowed to strap on his keytar for a solo in 'One Way Out', which is totally out of character for this guitar-based blues song. It almost derails the classic song entirely.

It was perhaps to everyone's relief that six months after the album's release, the band decided to throw in the towel again, following an appearance on *Saturday Night Live* on 23 January 1982. Gregg told the *Gainesville Sun* a few years later: 'I could tell that none of us were really enjoying it anymore. The money was still there, and the fans, but that didn't impress me. That may have been the worst time for me. That's when I decided to form my own band again. I had to get my music back and my health back'.

The band was to effectively split into two. In spring 1982, Allman took Dan Toler, David Toler and David Goldflies into a new iteration of The Gregg Allman Band. Betts recorded a solo album (unreleased) at Young'Un Sound in summer 1981, and performed live dates with Butch Trucks and Lawler and Cobb.

David Letterman interviewed Gregg on 25 January 1982. He sang 'Come And Go Blues' and introduced a magical, delicate version of 'Melissa' as 'the first song I ever wrote and kept'. What was once a memorial to his brother, was now, perhaps, a memorial to The Allman Brothers Band.

'Brothers Of The Road' (Dickey Betts, Jim Goff)
The title track lays down the album blueprint – professionally written and recorded, cleanly produced but displaying an air of desperation: everyone here is simply trying too hard. The chorus adds Doobie Brothers-style backing vocals, fiddle and slide gutar harmonies – like the whole album, it's pleasant enough, but offers nothing new.

'Leavin'' (Gregg Allman)
Gregg counts in a funky tune that has some clever syncopation. This track at least shows some commitment, with two very good guitar solos, and is so close to being the album's best song. It would've been fascinating to hear what the post-1989 band might've made of this. A real standout.

'Straight From The Heart' (Dickey Betts, Johnny Cobb)
Released as a single, 1981. Chart position: 39
Quite possibly the nadir of the band's output, this song is a horrible, commercial, slick AOR monstrosity, layered with synth pads, Hall and Oates-style backing vocals and trilling percussion. Gregg sounds utterly disconnected, and the harmony guitars sound flown in from another song.

The band played the song in concert, and, incredibly, mimed to the record on the Saturday night music show *Solid Gold*. This pushed it into the top 40, but it wasn't enough: this band was never a hit-singles machine. As Alan Paul writes in *One Way Out*: 'By then (they) were trudging along, trying hard to recapture a spark during an era that was just not interested'.

'The Heat Is On' (Dickey Betts, Mike Lawler, Buddy Yochim)
They performed this live in 1981. It has zero spark and no heat, is sub-reggae, with a long and very embarrassing rap ('I was born in the back woods, I was raised up like a slave/Having me a good time now is all I crave'), and co-wriitten with producer Mike Lawler and Dickey's long-time pal Buddy Yochim. Perhaps it's best if we all pretend that this doesn't exist.

'Maybe We Can Go Back To Yesterday' (Dickey Betts, Dan Toler)
Bright production, a half-decent Gregg vocal and a good Dan Toler guitar solo don't disguise the obvious attempt at a commercial pop song. It sounds nothing like The Allman Brothers Band.

'The Judgment' (Dickey Betts)
This is musically uninspired, despite a furious Betts solo, and is overworked lyrically: 'The cornered lion is not within the realm of reason/Fear is like the cracking of the lash'. Excuse me?

Performed live in 1981, 'The Judgement' extended to 15 minutes or more with tedious bass and drums solos.

'Two Rights' (Dickey Betts, John Cobb, Mike Lawler)
Released as a single, 1981. Did not chart.
'Two Rights' sounds like a late-period Doobie Brothers reject, with its swirling synthesizers, commercial chorus, trite lyric and mass backing vocals. This might be the worst song on ABB's worst album.

'Never Knew How Much (I Needed You)' (Gregg Allman)
And then – unexpectedly – a classic. Gregg puts his heart and soul into this excellent sincere ballad. He wrote it about his second wife Janice Blair, who also inspired 'Queen Of Hearts' on *Laid Back*.

It clearly meant a lot to Allman: performances in 1981 had grit and spirit. There's a stunning acoustic version with Betts and Toler in December 1981 as part of a short set, presumably for TV broadcast. Gregg is wasted, but his rough soulful growls are quite superb. He sings from his gut and you believe every word. You can (and should) watch this on YouTube.

An early demo of this song – recorded in September 1974 – is included on *One More Try: An Anthology* (1997).

'Things You Used To Do' (Gregg Allman, Keith England)

Swampy and funky, Gregg announced this as 'another song we wrote in desperation'. The production is more organic than some of the album's more-commercial numbers, so it's less rooted in 1981, and is all the better for that. The song was co-written with Keith England, who joined the Allman Brothers for six months as backing vocalist.

'I Beg Of You' (Rose Marie McCoy, Kelly Owens)

A cover of Elvis Presley's B-side to 'Don't' from 1958. Can you hear the sound of a barrel being scraped? By now, no one was listening.

Part III: 28 June 1989-7 May 2000

Dreams (1989)

Fast forward to 1989. Since *Brothers of the Road*, Lamar Williams – the band's bassist from 1972 to 1976 – had died from lung cancer: aged 34, in January 1983. That year, Betts, Leavell, Trucks and Goldflies teamed up with ex-Wet Willie vocalist/saxophonist Jimmy Hall, to form Betts, Hall, Leavell and Trucks. A young guitar player called Warren Haynes was sometimes a guest, along with his employer at the time: singer David Allen Coe.

Meanwhile, Gregg Allman formed a new iteration of his own band, with the Toler brothers and bassist Bruce Waibel. By 1985, Betts had his own four-piece, with Johnny Neel on keyboards.

Throughout most of 1986, The Dickey Betts Band and The Gregg Allman Band teamed up for an American tour that included a finale of both bands joining forces. While not technically an Allman Brothers Band reunion, audiences were receptive enough to warrant two official Allman Brothers Band shows that year. The first of these was on 12 July 1986 at Charlie Daniels' Volunteer Jam XII at the then-new Starwood Amphitheatre in Nashville. Other performers included Dobie Gray, The Judds, John 'Bo Duke' Schneider and Dwight Yoakam. The lineup was Allman, Betts, Jaimoe and Trucks, with Leavell and Dan Toler from previous lineups, along with bassist Bruce Waibel from The Gregg Allman Band. They played a 60-minute greatest-hits set comprising 'Statesboro Blues', 'Blue Sky', 'One Way Out', 'In Memory Of Elizabeth Reed', 'Ramblin' Man', 'Jessica' and 'Whipping Post'.

Three months later, the same lineup headlined Bill Graham's Crackdown anti-drug benefit at Madison Square Garden in New York, leading an eclectic bill that included Run-DMC, Santana, Ruben Blades, and Crosby, Stills & Nash. The Allmans' 45-minute set started at midnight and opened – appropriately enough – with 'Midnight Rider'. *The New York Times* reviewed the set:

> The Allman Brothers Band was in good form. The high point of Friday's set came in Dickey Betts' guitar solos with his ringing tone and slowly-spiralling phrases, and in the crossfire between the drummers. A shortened set meant that a band that made its reputation with extended jams, had to hold back.
> *The New York Times*, 2 November 1986

The set included a guest appearance by Paul Butterfield, just a few months before his death. Encores included a lively take on The Rascals' 'Good Lovin'' with guest and Rascals singer Felix Cavaliere, and a tired 'Key To The Highway' with Stephen Stills, Mick Taylor and Carlos Santana. The show was broadcast on WNEW, and is available on the grey market in excellent quality.

Buoyed by the warm welcome at these concerts, by Gregg's major success with his 1987 solo album *I'm No Angel,* and by the band's approaching 20th anniversary in March 1989, they reconvened for a concert tour to support a four-CD/six-album box set called *Dreams*. Across five hours and 55 songs, *Dreams* includes hard-to-find and/or first-time-on-CD tracks by The Allman Joys, Hour Glass, 31st of February and Second Coming, and solo material by Gregg Allman, Duane Allman and Dickey Betts. Previously unreleased (or very rare) Allman Brothers Band performances are listed here.

'Dreams' (Gregg Allman)

This demo of 'Dreams' was recorded at Capricorn in Macon in April 1969. It is less intense and more bluesy than the later New York take. This early version includes Dickey Betts' second guitar part, not later recorded for *The Allman Brothers Band*.

'Statesboro Blues' (Blind Willie McTell)

This is an outtake recorded for *Idlewild South* in February and July 1970. In his memoir, Gregg mentions another unidentified, unreleased studio take from August 1969.

'I'm Gonna Move To The Outskirts Of Town' (William Weldon, Roy Jordan)

This Little Milton song was often performed in the early days. This version is from the band's 11 April 1970 concert at Ludlow Garage in Cincinnati, and would've been a highlight of the set at that time. The entire concert has subsequently been made available in superb quality.

'One More Ride' (Gregg Allman, Dickey Betts)

This is a unique Allman/Betts composition; an incomplete instrumental outtake from *Idlewild South*. It has the basis of a classic Allmans song, and it's a shame it remained unfinished. A version with vocals circulates among collectors but is only for the most die-hard of fans (read as: not that good).

'Whipping Post' (Gregg Allman)
'In Memory of Elizabeth Reed' (Dickey Betts)

Remixes of the *At Fillmore East* versions.

'Drunken Hearted Boy' (Elvin Bishop)

The final encore from the fourth Filmore East concert, 13 March 1971.

'You Don't Love Me'/'Soul Serenade' (Live) (Willie Cobbs, Curtis Ousley, Luther Dixon)

Duane Allman plays tribute to the recently-deceased King Curtis, with a remarkable and wholly-improvised version of 'Soul Serenade' recorded before a small audience in New York City on 26 August 1971. This is proof – as if you needed it – of Allman's total mastery of his craft. It was later included on *Live from A&R Studios* (2016) and *Trouble No More: 50th Anniversary Collection* (2020).

'Blue Sky' (Dickey Betts)
'Little Martha' (Duane Allman)
'Melissa' (Gregg Allman)
1988 remixes of the *Eat a Peach* recordings. Gregg's sublime Hammond B3-playing is higher in the mix on 'Blue Sky', and 'Little Martha' includes a previously-unheard bass part.

'Ain't Wastin' Time No More' (Gregg Allman)
A live recording by the five-piece band from Puerto Rico in April 1972 – released on *Mar y Sol: The First International Puerto Rico Pop Festival* in November 1972.

'One Way Out' (Elmore James, Marshall Sehorn, Sonny Boy Williamson II)
This unreleased live track from Winterland, San Francisco, 26 September 1973 is from the recordings that gave us *Wipe the Windows, Check the Oil, Dollar Gas*. The entire concert was made available as part of the 2013 Super Deluxe Edition of *Brothers And Sisters*.

'Just Ain't Easy' (Gregg Allman)
An alternative studio version of a song from *Enlightened Rogues* (1979).

'In Memory Of Elizabeth Reed' (Dickey Betts)
A rare live recording from 19 July 1979 (one of only two that are officially available), this is from the Merriweather Pavilion in Columbia, Maryland. The entire set from Nassau Coliseum on 30 December 1979 was broadcast by WLIR, and has been released in various formats over the years.

Gregg Allman fans should also enjoy a cover of The Beatles' 'Rain' recorded with the Charles May Ensemble in 1985, that owes much to Ray Charles (The Allman Brothers Band performed this from time to time in 2013-2014), and the 1977 duet 'Can You Fool' with Gregg's then-wife Cher. There's also Betts' unreleased 'Nancy' from 1981, and 'Duane's Tune': a June 1988 instrumental by The Dickey Betts Band.

Always intriguing and totally worthwhile, the *Dreams* box set was compiled by Bill Levenson, who'd put together Eric Clapton's successful *Crossroads* box set in 1988.

Dreams was released on 20 June 1989, and a week later, the band was back on the road with an important new member: Warren Haynes. Haynes had worked with the uncompromising country singer David Allan Coe between 1980 and 1984, and was lead guitarist in blues and roots band The Nighthawks in the mid-1980s: replacing Jimmy Nalls (ex-Sea Level). Radio Forrest interviewed Haynes in 2019:

I met Dickey Betts when I was very young; I think I was 20 when I met those guys. And I was a big Allman Brothers fan. A few years later, when the Allman Brothers were broken up, I had gotten hired to be a background vocalist on the recording that Dickey Betts was making in Nashville, and when I walked into the studio, he was like, 'Oh man, good to see you. You got a guitar with you?'. I was like, 'No', but we kinda rekindled our friendship, and shortly after that, he called me and said he wanted to put a band together, and we started writing songs together and wound up making his record *Pattern Disruptive*, which was in 1988. And then in 1989, he called me and asked me to join the Allman Brothers for what was going to be a reunion tour. There was the 20th anniversary, and it was just going to be one year, but it was very successful and everybody was getting along and the band sounded great, so we just kind of kept doing it.

Haynes toured with The Dickey Betts Band in 1988 and sang lead on classic Allman Brothers Band songs such as 'Statesboro Blues' and 'One Way Out'. He also appears on 'Duane's Tune' on the *Dreams* box set. Haynes told *The Georgia Straight* in 1994:

The whole time that we played together in (Betts') band, there was never any indication that the Allman Brothers would get back together. If the topic was ever brought up, nobody was really excited about it. But then things kinda started comin' around. Stevie Ray Vaughan was gaining some momentum, as was Robert Cray, and things started headin' back towards the blues a little bit. I think as that started happening, Dickey and Gregg and Butch and Jaimoe all got together and thought, 'Hey, maybe it's time we buried the hatchet'.

Gregg admitted:

One positive was Warren Haynes, because he served as kind of an anchor for Dickey. Warren was Dickey's choice as the other guitar player: it was a package deal. That was Dickey's choice to make, because I sure wasn't going to do it. I had met Warren earlier – around '86 or so – and I liked him right away. I liked what he brought to the table, because he could play, write and sing, so he helped make it desirable to put the band back together.

Butch Trucks explained to *Los Angeles Times* in 1995:

Warren came in and filled a spot. When we put this back together, we decided to go back to the double guitar. We didn't do that right after Duane's death, for obvious reasons. But now it's 20 years later, and we felt like it was time to go back to doing things the way we started them. Warren is absolutely perfect. He plays a great slide guitar, and he has his own style. He's been up there these past six years, and he still sounds like Warren Haynes.

Haynes said, 'Had I not worked with Dickey, I would've had more trouble adapting. Duane was a great player, and he died young, and those two things lead people to immortalise him, so I know some people in the audience would like me to play like Duane Allman. But, for my sake, I just can't do that'.

Trucks said, 'We just about had to beat Warren up to get him to play that signature lick on 'Statesboro Blues', because he didn't want to copy Duane. He's very much an individual'.

The new lineup was completed by keyboard player Johnny Neel and bassist Allen Woody. Neel had played with The Dickey Betts Band. Gregg was forthright with his opinion: 'I really didn't like having him in the band. Dickey wanted him and I went along with it, because it did save me from playing a lot of stuff I didn't want to play anyway'. On the tour, Neel got a solo lead vocal on 'Blues Ain't Nothin'': a track from Betts' 1988 album *Pattern Disruptive*. Allen Woody had been a member of The Artimus Pyle Band (led by the former Lynyrd Skynyrd drummer Artimus Pyle) in the mid-1980s. Pyle introduced Woody to Butch Trucks, who suggested that Woody audition as bassist for ABB. Gregg:

I had never really done a full-blown audition, and I hated it doing it this far down the line. Just through word of mouth, something like 11 bass players showed up. We played the same three songs all day long: 'One Way Out', 'Dreams' and 'Whipping Post'. There was (a) dude with real long hair who had four basses lined up: just beautiful machines. He sat over in the corner, waiting to be last. Well, that was Allen Woody. Just the way he grabbed his shit and plugged it in – he had this air about him. He had a very confident look, which is just what we wanted. All through the other auditions, I kept looking at him. Before he even played a note, I thought, 'That's him'.

Woody stayed with the band for eight years. Gregg Allman told *Hittin' The Note*:

They're not sidemen, that's for sure. They are Allman Brothers – much more so than some people in earlier incarnations. And that's a big difference.

Seven Turns (1990)

Personnel:

Gregg Allman: Hammond B3 organ, lead vocals ('Good Clean Fun', 'Low Down Dirty Mean', 'Shine It On', 'Gambler's Roll', 'It Ain't Over Yet'), backing vocals ('Seven Turns')

Dickey Betts: electric and acoustic guitar, National resonator guitar, lead vocals ('Let Me Ride', 'Seven Turns')

Warren Haynes: electric guitar, lead vocals ('Loaded Dice'), backing vocals ('Let Me Ride', 'Shine It On', 'Seven Turns', 'It Ain't Over Yet')

Jaimoe: drums, percussion

Johnny Neel: piano, Wurlitzer organ, synthesizer, harmonica, backing vocals ('Shine It On', 'Seven Turns', 'It Ain't Over Yet')

Butch Trucks: drums, timpani

Allen Woody: bass

Mark Morris: percussion

Duane Betts: guitar ('True Gravity')

Recorded April 1990 at Criteria Studios, Miami, Florida

Producer: Tom Dowd

Release date: July 1990

Chart position: 53

There was a lot riding on *Seven Turns*, the Allman Brothers' first album in nine years. Warren Haynes and Allen Woody were wise and crucial band additions alongside the four founder members. Tom Dowd signed on as producer, and the band returned to Criteria in Miami, where they.d worked with Dowd on *Idlewild South*, *Eat A Peach* and *Enlightened Rogues*.

Seven Turns sees a band in transition. Gregg Allman receives only one co-writing credit, compared to seven for Betts and four for Haynes. But the music is full of muscle and grit with the occasional wistful elegance.

The late-1980s saw a revival in the fortunes of bands of the early-1970s, so the Allmans' timing was apposite, and their ninth studio album presented a group of veteran musicians proving they could still do what they did best. *Seven Turns* went a long way towards restoring their reputation.

Warren Haynes told *Billboard* in 2020:

When (Allman and Betts) began to see that classic-rock revival in the late-'80s, not only did they realise they were fitting in again, but they were forever proven timeless at that point. I think when the band reformed for *Seven Turns*, what they discovered was that their music was timeless and, from that point forward, would always be looked at that way.

Meanwhile, midway through the sessions, Butch Trucks took Gregg Allman, Allen Woody and Warren Haynes to a gig at a small club called Tropics International in South Beach, Miami. Gregg:

So we're sitting there, and they announced the band back on, and they said, 'Derek Trucks'. Butchie looks over and gives us a shit-eatin' grin, and says, 'Wait till you see who it is'. I said, 'That's your nephew – that's your (sister's) kid'. And he said, 'Yep, that's my nephew, but hang on to what you got when he puts that guitar on'. They came in and put on their gear, and Derek was just barely taller than that Gibson. He started with that slide – matter of fact, slide was all he knew how to play at that time, and I thought, 'Well, that's a first'. But he blew the roof off that place. I said, 'Man, how old is this guy?'. Butch said, 'Well, he's ten'.

'Good Clean Fun' (Gregg Allman, Dickey Betts, Johnny Neel)
Released as a single, 1991. Chart position: 1 (US Mainstream)
Boom! 'Good Clean Fun' is the musical equivalent of a shot across the bows, with barely-contained power, initially restrained, then brilliantly unleashed as the guitar solos potently lift the song.

The group promoted *Seven Turns* on *The Tonight Show Starring Johnny Carson* in October 1991, performing this and 'True Gravity'. They were back, finally.

'Let Me Ride' (Dickey Betts)
Country-tinged with delicate guitar harmonies, 'Let Me Ride' places Dickey's thin vocal way back in the mix. But as a vehicle for Betts' and Haynes' lead guitars, this is a perfect album track.

'Low Down Dirty Mean' (Dickey Betts, Johnny Neel)
This is a classic off-kilter blues, with slide guitar, harmonica and a seriously impressive vocal turn from gruntin' Gregg. It's an obvious mash-up of Ruth Brown's 'Mama, He Treats Your Daughter Mean' and Muddy Waters' 'Hoochie Coochie Man', and includes perhaps one too many of the common blues cliches.

But with astounding playing like this, who cares?

'Shine It On' (Dickey Betts, Warren Haynes)
'I've had my troubles', groans Gregg. Too right. 'Shine It On' though, has a much-needed optimism.

Before you end up out there on your own
Don't let some rainy day steal your heart away
You got to go on
It's just the dark before the dawn
Shine It On

Haynes' short sharp guitar solo is terrific.

'Loaded Dice' (Dickey Betts, Warren Haynes)

Warren Haynes sings this swinging mid-tempo blues shuffle with power and conviction, and also adds some mean slide guitar. The slide solo is sublime, and the lyrics add a twist to the 'mean woman' trope.

Well the first time that I saw you
Said you'd just dumped your old man
Then the next time you was dealin'
Must have dealt me a losing hand
Woman I tried to win your love
Just can't pay the price
Keep throwing in sevens
I keep on playing with loaded dice

Haynes' singing and playing sits right in the pocket, and he is established here as a crucial second-act member of The Allman Brothers Band.

'Seven Turns' (Dickey Betts)

Released as a single, 1991. Chart position: 12 (US Mainstream).
Betts wrote the lovely 'Seven Turns' after producer Tom Dowd asked him to create something similar to 'Blue Sky'. The acoustic-based 'Seven Turns' refers to a Navajo belief that there are seven times in life that you must make a decision that determines your life path: just as 'Blue Sky celebrated Betts' Native Canadian girlfriend Sandy 'Bluesky'.

It's a country rocker, and features Haynes' slide and Betts' tight lead lines.

The call-and-response vocals came about when Gregg Allman was shooting pool as Haynes and Betts worked out vocal harmonies. Gregg answered their vocal lines, and the idea stuck. Tasty slide guitar plays out this excellent song.

'Gambler's Roll' (Warren Haynes, Johnny Neel)

This loud, impressive slow blues in 6/8 is the album centrepiece and lays the blueprint for the rest of the band's studio output – exquisitely written, brilliantly performed; Gregg and Warren in top form. Finally, everything the band had been moving towards since imploding in 1976 was back in place. Warren Haynes' place in the band was his, for as long as he wanted it.

'True Gravity' (Dickey Betts, Warren Haynes)

This is a soaring eight-minute instrumental epic; complex and twisting, wholly satisfying: a 'Liz Reed' for the 1990s. Dickey's 11-year-old son Duane Betts adds guitar, Johnny Neel channels Chuck Leavell, and Butch bangs his timpani. Classic stuff.

During the band's summer-1996 shows, this song could extend to 30 minutes or more, in true 'Mountain Jam' style.

'True Gravity' was nominated as Best Rock Instrumental Performance at the 33rd annual Grammy awards, losing to 'D/FW' by Stevie Ray and Jimmie Vaughan.

'It Ain't Over Yet' (Doug Crider, Johnny Neel)
Released as a single, 1991. Chart position: 26 (US Mainstream)
Co-written by Johnny Neel with Suzy Boguss' husband Doug Crider, the bullish and uplifting 'It Ain't Over Yet' ends the album with a crooked groove. Woody's bass, pops; Neel's piano, jives, and the singers harmonise: all brought together as a wonderful end to a very good album.

Shades of Two Worlds (1991)

Personnel:
Gregg Allman: Hammond B3 organ, piano, lead vocals
Dickey Betts: lead, rhythm and acoustic guitar
Warren Haynes: lead, rhythm, slide and acoustic guitar, background vocals
Jaimoe: drums, percussion, background vocals
Marc Quiñones: percussion
Butch Trucks: drums, percussion, background vocals
Allen Woody: bass
Recorded April 1991 at Ardent Recording, Memphis, Tennessee
Producer: Tom Dowd
Release date: July 1991
Chart position: 85

Shades of Two Worlds expands on the promise of *Seven Turns*. With Warren Haynes firmly at the helm (he co-writes more than half the songs here), Gregg was able to concentrate on singing and performing. Dickey Betts also turned in some strong songs – 'Nobody Knows' in particular – but also a couple of clunkers, in 'Desert Blues' and 'Midnight Man'.

The album sessions introduced percussionist Marc Quiñones. He worked as a session player on the album for only two days but was asked to join the band for their 1991 summer tour. Quiñones had performed and/or recorded with Willie Colón, Rubén Blades, David Byrne and jazz fusion band Spyro Gyra. His tenure in ABB lasted for more than 23 years. Johnny Neel had left the band the previous year.

'End Of The Line' (Gregg Allman, Warren Haynes, Allen Woody, John Jaworowicz)
Released as a single, 1991. Chart position: 2 (US Mainstream)
The band's second 1990s album continued their rejuvenation, and delivered strong original material. Allman, Haynes, and Woody wrote the song with John Jaworowicz of Blues Collective. Jaworowicz and Haynes had co-written the title track of Gregg Allman's 1988 album *Before The Bullets Fly*.

'End Of The Line' is a classic album opener with pulsing dynamics. Gregg's vocal conveys authenticity, the performance has a beautifully light touch, and everything comes together perfectly. 'Life ain't what it seems in the boulevard of broken dreams', Gregg grumbles. Amen.

'Bad Rain' (Dickey Betts, Warren Haynes)
Gregg sings a troubles-of-my-own song. 'Bad Rain' pushes hard, with a powerful chorus, a syncopated breakdown, some nifty jazz changes, a stinging overdriven Haynes slide guitar solo, and some smooth playing from Dickey Betts.

'Nobody Knows' (Dickey Betts)
Dickey Betts: 'Tom Dowd had said, 'We could use a tune as heavy as 'Whipping Post" for this record', and I thought, 'Man, that's a tall order!''.

'Nobody Knows' is a *tour de force*. Yes, it's a rewrite of 'Whipping Post' (both songs are in A minor with a 12/8 rhythm), but 'Nobody Knows' is as powerful a track as any in the band's history. Betts said, ''Nobody Knows' is one of the best lyrical songs I've ever written. These are nice, abstract, poetic lyrics. I wrote that about as fast as I could write the words down, at 4:30 in the morning after rehearsal. I sat down and those words just started flying out. In 30 minutes, I'd written the whole thing, like I was writing a letter to someone'.

There is an inherent power in the performance – that peerless rhythm section drives the song, Allen Woody's bass licks underpinning everything. Then at 5:16 everything drops to a whisper. Dickey shines, as his fluid solo urges the band to build back up through a remarkable midsection that's as good an anything on *At Fillmore East*, despite the ghosts of 'Whipping Post' floating above. There is real fire in the belly here. 'Nobody Knows' might be an homage, but it's a good one.

'Desert Blues' (Dickey Betts, Warren Haynes)
An anti-Iraq-War song sung by Dickey Betts, which is far too-close-for-comfort to the flag-waving of Lynyrd Skynyrd.

> Sand in my collar
> Got the sand in my hair
> Got it in my pockets
> Got it everywhere
> I got sand in my shirt
> Got it in my shoes
> Got them low-down, dried-out desert blues

Sure, Skynyrd has its place, but not here.

'Get On With Your Life' (Gregg Allman)
Gregg sings the blues. There's a woman involved, of course.

> It's the same as the times you laughed in my face
> Won't somebody please wake me from this bad dream
> I remember my grandmama told me
> Things ain't always what they seem
> So get on with your life baby
> Please let me get on with mine

The guitars weep and wail, the rhythm section keeps it subtle, and Gregg's vocal is hurt and defiant in equal measure. Bliss.

'Midnight Man' (Dickey Betts, Warren Haynes)
Perhaps the album's weakest song, 'Midnight Man' is a pumping rocker, sung by Gregg, to a strong riff. It offers nothing new, but sits comfortably amongst the better songs elsewhere.

'Kind Of Bird' (Dickey Betts, Warren Haynes)
This pumped-up jazz/blues instrumental was written in honour of jazz legend Charlie 'Bird' Parker. Again, the useless 'southern rock' label can be dismissed – no one else played music like this: a complex, vibrant companion piece to 'In Memory Of Elizabeth Reed'. After laying down the main theme, the band stretch out, with an organ solo from Gregg, and Warren and Dickey's guitar solos, repeating the main theme after each section. There's also a brief nod to Jimi Hendrix' 'Foxy Lady'. At 5:17, the song breaks down into an astonishing free-form section which sounds like the Grateful Dead on mescalin. The main theme returns for a triumphant finale.

Marc Quiñones and Allen Woody deserve kudos for their tight playing throughout.

'Kind Of Bird' was nominated for Best Rock Instrumental at the 34th Grammy Awards in 1991. It has often been included in setlists of Hayne's band Gov't Mule.

'Come On in My Kitchen' (Robert Johnson; Arr. Dickey Betts)
This starts as a faithful reworking of Robert Johnson's 1937 song, with a typically regretful Gregg Allman brimming with blues and soul. The second verse ups the tempo to a full-band country blues with a gospel choir and some devastating guitar picking. And no drums. There is also a sly musical quote from Johnson's 'Hot Tamales (They're Red Hot)', for good measure.

An Evening with the Allman Brothers Band: First Set (1992)

Personnel:

Gregg Allman: Hammond B3 organ, piano, acoustic guitar, lead vocals
Dickey Betts: lead, rhythm, acoustic, acoustic slide guitar, lead vocals
Warren Haynes: lead, rhythm, slide, acoustic guitar, background vocals
Jaimoe: drums, background vocals
Marc Quiñones: percussion
Butch Trucks: drums, timpani, background vocals
Allen Woody: bass, 5 string fretless bass, 18-string bass, acoustic bass, background vocals
Thom Doucette: harmonica
Recorded December 1991 at Macon City Auditorium, Macon, Georgia; 3-4 March 1992 at Orpheum Theatre, Boston, Massachusetts; 10-11 March 1992 at Beacon Theatre, New York Producer: Tom Dowd
Release date: June 1992
Chart position: 80

This is the first of two live albums from the 1990s-era band, released three years apart. The playing is nothing short of magnificent. The only new song here is 'Midnight Blues' – a slow, gentle acoustic reworking of Blind Willie McTell's 'Blues At Midnight', with mostly-new lyrics by Dickey Betts and a mellow harmonica solo by Thom Doucette. The versions of 'Get On With Your Life' and 'Nobody Knows' (both from *Shades of Two Worlds*) are compelling and electrifying.

Tracklist:

1. 'End Of The Line', 2. 'Blue Sky', 3. 'Get On With Your Life', 4. 'Southbound', 5. 'Midnight Blues', 6. 'Melissa', 7. 'Nobody Knows', 8. 'Dreams', 9. 'Revival'

Where It All Begins (1994)

Personnel:
Gregg Allman: organ, lead vocals
Dickey Betts: lead guitar, lead vocals
Warren Haynes: lead guitar, lead vocals
Jaimoe: drums, percussion
Marc Quiñones: percussion
Butch Trucks: drums
Allen Woody: bass
Recorded January 1994 at BR Ranch Studios, Jupiter, Florida
Producer: Tom Dowd
Release date: May 1994
Chart position: 45

Despite the band's stable lineup since 1989, they were faced with their usual personal issues. Gregg:

> Still, there were problems, only this time they didn't have a thing to do with me. Now it was Dickey heading off the tracks. *Where It All Begins* was the last studio album we ever did with Dickey, because both his behaviour and his playing were becoming more erratic, and issues developed between him and Allen Woody. Basically, Woody was tired of taking Dickey's shit, and it got pretty ugly between them. Warren too had grown weary of Dickey's subpar playing and the fact that Dickey's solution was to just crank it up and play even louder.

Dickey Betts was arrested the day after a show in Saratoga Springs, New York, on 30 July 1993. Officers responded to a call from Dickey's wife saying he was drunk and abusive, when the guitarist decided to shove the policemen, leading to his arrest. Betts flew home, and Jimmy Herring of Aquarium Rescue Unit sat in for that night's show. With Herring unavailable for the rest of the tour, the band needed to find an answer at very short notice. Storyville guitarist David Grissom was called, but was unavailable for the following night's show in Mansfield, Massachusetts. Ex-Ozzy Osbourne guitarist Zakk Wylde was the unlikely next option. Wylde lasted one night, and Grissom filled in for the next two weeks, starting on 3 August in Columbia, Maryland. Future ABB-er Jack Pearson played at the final nine shows. Betts entered a Florida rehab centre in 1994.
Warren Haynes spoke to *The Georgia Straight* in 1994:

> Having gone through the '80s, I think people are realizing that a lot of music during that time was headed away from what we refer to as real music. Machines are great for making demos and for writing songs, and technology is a wonderful outlet, but at the same time, some of the best music ever

made was made on a $40 guitar with a human voice. So the music starts inside, and you translate it to the audience. It doesn't always take 64 tracks of digital technology to do that. And that's kind of the premise behind *Where It All Begins*. That record was done like an old record, where everything was recorded live on the fly.

Indeed, the album was recorded in a week at Burt Reynolds' ranch in Jupiter, Florida, following three weeks of intense rehearsals. It was the third album in the band's 1990s comeback: all recorded in an intense four-year period. The band continued to tour, but it would be nine years until their next (and final) studio album.

'All Night Train' (Gregg Allman, Warren Haynes, Chuck Leavell)
Haynes' picturesque slide guitar, colours a tired song dealing with drug addiction. Gregg Allman's life experiences are clear in direct verses such as the below:

I woke up late yesterday afternoon
My eyeballs feeling like two balloons
The doctor say things ain't never gonna change
Till you stop riding that all-night train

'Sailin' 'Cross The Devil's Sea' (Gregg Allman, Warren Haynes, Allen Woody, Jack Pearson)
This was written during four-way composing sessions at Gregg Allman's house. Jack Pearson had toured as a member of the band in summer 1993, and also performed with Johnny Neel and the Last Word (1994-1995) and Gregg Allman and Friends (1995-1997).

Pearson explained to *Hittin' The Note* in 1997: 'When we wrote ('Sailin' 'Cross The Devil's Sea'), I was playing a dobro, sittin' around Gregg's kitchen table. We had this groove going, and I would play a lick between the vocals. Later they took that lick and developed into this powerful thing'.

And powerful is the right word. Allman and the band are energetic and completely focused.

A second song from these writing sessions – 'Rockin' Horse' – was a highlight of Gov't Mule's 1995 debut album, and the Allman Brothers recorded it for their final album *Hittin' The Note*.

'Back Where It All Begins' (Dickey Betts)
Released as a single, 1994. Chart position: 29 (US Mainstream)
A late-period Betts classic, with a very *live* feel, but with inevitable echoes of 'Jessica', 'Revival' and 'Blue Sky' in its composition and delivery. It's worth it for the long guitar solo from 1:37 to 6:17; with another from 7:12 to the end of the song.

'Soulshine' (Warren Haynes)

'Soulshine' – surely Warren Haynes' best song – was first recorded in 1993 by blues musician Larry McCray. Readers are urged to track down McCray's album *Delta Hurricane*: his scintillating version joins blues to gospel, to brilliant effect.

Haynes clearly recognised the song's strength. This outstanding Allman Brothers version is nothing less than a classic, as sung by Gregg, with a rare tone of hope.

When you can't find the light to guide you through a cloudy day
When the stars ain't shinin' bright, you feel like you've lost your way
When the candlelight of home burns so very far away
You gotta let your soul shine, just like my daddy used to say

Haynes said in 1994: 'My dad was a big influence and inspiration to me. Not that he's a musician, because he's not, but he has this natural singing talent that he was never given a chance to pursue. He could see early on that I was obsessed with music, really, and he encouraged me to follow my heart and my dream'.

When Haynes and Allen Woody formed Gov't Mule, they took the song with them and released their own stellar versions on *The Deep End, Volume 1* (with session ace Willie Weeks on bass, Dave Matthews Band's Tim Reynold on guitar, Chuck Leavell on organ, and Little Milton singing it as a duet) and *The Deepest End, Live in Concert*.

The song's durability was confirmed by Beth Hart covering it on her 2007 album *37 Days,* and by its inclusion in Allman Brothers Band's live setlists for 20 years.

'No One To Run With' (Dickey Betts, John Prestia)

Released as a single, 1994. Chart position: 7 (US Mainstream)
As early as 1994, Dickey Betts was acutely aware of his mortality. Duane Allman, Berry Oakley and Lamar Williams had already died, and 'No One To Run With' reworks 'Revival' with a message about leaving the past behind and starting a new life. Haynes slides, Dickey picks, and Trucks and Jaimoe pound out the Bo Diddley beat. Gregg Allman sings the song, and it stayed in the live set long after Betts' departure: all the way through to 2014. The live version from *Second Set* is terrific. The co-writer was Nashville-based guitarist John Prestia.

'Change My Way Of Living' (Dickey Betts)

Betts wrote this pumped-up blues about his need to modify his lifestyle before it killed him. 'Blue, Lord I'm blue', he sings. 'Raining down on me'. Betts' solo replicates the simple pentatonic scale of 'Statesboro Blues', and Haynes adds bright slide guitar.

'Mean Woman Blues' (Dickey Betts)
Not the Roy Orbison song, but a fierce, driving blues-rocker sung by Warren Haynes. Apparently a 1994 version of 'Rockin' Horse' was bumped off the album for this: oh well.

'Everybody's Got A Mountain To Climb' (Dickey Betts)
This Betts song is mid-tempo and cheesy, but such was the skill of this iteration of the band that they could rise above the occasional cliché:

> Hey let me tell you what I'm talkin' about
> You can't go around with your lip stuck out
> Life ain't all good but it sure ain't bad
> Anyway it's the best old life I ever had

The chorus ramps up soulful backing vocals to terrific effect. The delivery is strong, even when the message is trite.

'What's Done Is Done' (Gregg Allman, Allen Woody)
This displays all the standard Allman Brothers tropes recognizable from tracks such as 'Don't Keep Me Wonderin'' and 'Good Clean Fun'. This is familiar musical territory; excellently performed, but offering nothing new.

'Temptation Is A Gun' (Gregg Allman, Jonathan Cain, Neal Schon)
A slow-burning blues, written with Jonathan Cain and Neal Schon of Californian rock band Journey. It borrows heavily from the Grateful Dead's 1990s version of 'The Same Thing'. Don't listen too hard to the preaching lyric.

Thursday 12 January 1995, The Waldorf, New York City, NY

The original six band members were inducted into the Rock and Roll Hall of Fame in 1995, along with Al Green, Janis Joplin, Led Zeppelin, Martha and the Vandellas, Neil Young and Frank Zappa. Gregg wrote in his memoir:

I arrived in New York on a Sunday, got drunk, and stayed drunk for five days. I remember little bits – flashes of this and that – of the week that ultimately changed my life; the ceremony in the ballroom of the Waldorf. One of my old buddies called me, and ... (next) thing you know, I was at the lobby bar. 'C'mon, man, let me buy you a drink'. They started collecting in front of me, from people all around the bar. Needless to say, I sat there and got shit-faced. One thing I'd been concerned about beforehand was my acceptance speech. There were a lot of things I wanted to say ... but instead, I just got up there and said, 'This is for my brother. He was always the first to face the fire. Thank you'. That's about all I could get out, and it was one of the most embarrassing moments of my life. I had just won the highest award there is in my profession, and I didn't give a damn; I just wanted another drink. It was so pathetic, but I remember thinking, 'You are better than this, and it's time for this crap to stop'. I knew it was time for a change.

It took a few years, but to his credit, Allman *did* sober up, and the band were about to hit their second peak.

An Evening with the Allman Brothers Band: 2nd Set (1995)

Personnel:
Gregg Allman: Hammond B3 organ, acoustic guitar, lead vocals
Dickey Betts: lead, rhythm and acoustic guitar, lead vocals
Warren Haynes: lead, rhythm, slide and acoustic guitar, lead and background vocals
Jaimoe: drums, percussion, background vocals
Marc Quiñones: percussion
Butch Trucks: drums, timpani, background vocals
Allen Woody: bass, fretless bass, 6-string bass, acoustic bass, background vocals
Recorded at R&R Club in Los Angeles, CA, June 1992; Walnut Creek Amphitheatre, Raleigh, NC, July 1994; Garden State Arts Center, Holmdel, NJ, August 1994
Producer: Tom Dowd
Release date: May 1995
Chart position: 88

2nd Set combines some well-chosen classics with four tracks from *Where It All Begins*, and a cover of Willie Dixon's 'The Same Thing' sung by Warren Haynes, which receives its first release here. Here is a band absolutely back at their best. The version of 'No One to Run With' is perhaps definitive, with a great Allen Woody bass line, soaring Haynes/Betts guitar parts and a rumbling Allman vocal. 'In Memory Of Elizabeth Rebed' is performed in a remarkable all-acoustic arrangement.

The album received good reviews, with *The Los Angeles Times*' Buddy Siegal singling Warren Haynes out for praise on 1 July 1995:

Many believe that Haynes in particular, is largely responsible for (the band's) resurgence. A series of inferior guitarists who came in the wake of Duane Allman's death, never really compensated for his loss, musically or spiritually. The soaring dual-guitar harmonies of Allman and Betts – which defined the group's original sound – wasn't recaptured until Haynes was recruited. And in Haynes, the Allmans found not only a guitarist who worked well with Betts, but also a creative, passionate player with a vision of his own; a musician with a voice and gift that kept pace with the group's ambitious, journeying jams.

Tracklist:
1. 'Sailin' 'Cross the Devil's Sea', 2. 'You Don't Love Me', 3. 'Soulshine', 4. 'Back Where It All Begins', 5. 'In Memory Of Elizabeth Reed', 6. 'The Same Thing', 7. 'No One To Run With', 8. 'Jessica'

The album received two Grammy nominations in 1996. 'Jessica' won Best Rock Instrumental Performance, and – bizarrely – 'In Memory Of Elizabeth Reed' was nominated for Best Pop Instrumental Performance.

Peakin' at the Beacon (2000)

Personnel:
Gregg Allman: organ, piano, acoustic guitar, vocals
Dickey Betts: guitar, vocals
Oteil Burbridge: bass
Jaimoe: drums, percussion
Marc Quiñones: conga, percussion, vocals
Butch Trucks: drums, percussion
Derek Trucks: guitar
Recorded March 2000 at the Beacon Theatre, New York City
Producers: The Allman Brothers Band
Release date: November 2000
Chart position: did not chart

The period 1997 to 2000 saw great upheaval within the band. In March 1997, Warren Haynes and Allen Woody left the group after eight years. Gregg Allman: 'Warren and Allen wanted to devote more time to Gov't Mule, so they decided to split the band after the '97 Beacon run. I was bummed to see them go, but I completely got it'.

Allen was replaced by Oteil Burbridge, and Haynes by guitarist Jack Pearson. Burbridge was the bassist in Aquarium Rescue Unit from 1989, alongside Jimmy Herring. That band had shared concert dates with the Allman Brothers Band and Gov't Mule, and in spring 1997, Burbridge and Herring were invited to join Butch Trucks' jazz/rock/calypso/metal fusion jam band Frogwings, for a series of concerts in late May. Derek Trucks and Marc Quiñones were also part of Frogwings, as were vocalist Edwin McCain and flautist Kofi Burbridge. Butch Trucks subsequently invited Oteil to audition, and within three weeks, he was in the band and on the road. Burbridge said in 1997: 'This group needs a bassist who is a jazz player with an understanding of rock and roll, or rock player who understands jazz. I'm combining my experiences in both types of music, and I'm funnelling it all through Berry Oakley. He is my guide through this whole thing'. Burbridge's attitude ensured him a place in The Allman Brothers Band for the next 17 years.

Jack Pearson moved across from Gregg Allman's solo band. He had filled in for an absent Dickey Betts in The Allman Brothers Band for three weeks in 1993. Pearson said in 1997:

I knew Warren from when he lived in Nashville. We had done some jamming together. I'd sit in with his band, and he'd sit in with mine. Warren called me right away when Dickey had to leave, but I couldn't get out of some commitments I had made. They ended up using (other guitarists) until I could go out with them. I flew into Dallas, Warren and I went into the hotel room, and we worked out the harmony parts, and then we went out and played.

These dates led to Pearson touring with Gregg Allman, and ultimately to a full-time gig with ABB. He toured with the band for almost two years, but only one official recording has been released – Pearson's showcase 'I'm Not Crying': recorded at the Beacon in March 1999 and included in the *Trouble No More* box set.

For two gigs in August 1998, Pearson was replaced by 19-year-old Derek Trucks, and when Pearson left in March 1999 at the end of that year's Beacon run, Trucks joined full-time. Warren Haynes: 'From the beginning, Derek had *the touch* – the tone, vibrato, note selection – he had just what it takes to be a great player from the very first. When he used to come out and sit in with the Allman Brothers, the first ten seconds of Derek's solo would garner the biggest applause of the night'.

Trucks said in 1999: 'When I first started playing guitar, I keyed in to Duane. He really cut through me and put me on the path of listening to music and the possibilities and power of what it can do. A lot of times – right before I'm about to do a Duane solo – there is a lot of energy in the air. It's a pretty heavy thing for me to look up and see the same players and hear those sounds that I first heard so many years ago'.

Gregg Allman:

Do I believe in reincarnation? After seeing Derek Trucks, how could I not? People ask me about Derek and my brother all the time, and I usually give them a little generic answer, because it's a pretty heavy question. But I have very good peripheral vision, and sometimes I'll catch him out of the corner of my eye, and the way he stands looks just like my brother. Anybody who knows Derek Trucks will tell you that he would be the last one in line to be accused of trying to look like somebody else. Derek is Derek, man. He puts on a pair of Levi's and a t-shirt, plugs his guitar into the amp, and plays. That was my brother, man.

The word 'prodigy' could've been coined for Derek Trucks. In 1988 – aged nine – he bought a $5 guitar at a garage sale, and by late 1989 he was working clubs in Jacksonville. He first performed with Gregg Allman, Butch Trucks, Woody and Haynes when they sat in at one of his shows at a small venue in Miami Beach in April 1990. Three months later, he appeared on stage with The Allman Brothers Band, and toured in 1991 as support act for Aquarium Rescue Unit: a band that included future ABB members Oteil Burbridge and Jimmy Herring.

Derek Trucks formed his own band in 1992, and toured in support of Lynyrd Skynyrd, The Gregg Allman Band and Gov't Mule. He told the *Miami Times* in 2018: 'My family never travelled, so it was great seeing the world. It was weird being on the road and having all these girls screaming at me, and then having to go back to high school in Jacksonville the next week'. Derek Trucks played live with Frogwings in 1997, 1998 and 1999: with Butch Trucks, Oteil

101

Burbridge, Marc Quiñones and Jimmy Herring. Now deemed ready, Derek was signed on for the Allman Brothers' 1999 summer tour, which began in Colorado in June and ran across the US until mid-September.

On their 1999 tour, the band alternated between two sets. They opened with either 'Don't Want You No More/It's Not My Cross to Bear' or 'True Gravity' (from *Seven Turns*), and included the new Betts instrumental 'JJ's Alley', a short acoustic set (usually 'Seven Turns' and 'Melissa'), and newer songs such as 'Sailin' 'Cross The Devil's Sea', 'Change My Way Of Living', 'End Of The Line' and 'Back Where It All Begins'. Their encore was usually the mighty 'No One To Run With'.

The following year, the band's regular residency at New York's Beacon Theatre comprised 13 sold-out dates. 'Mountain Jam' was performed for the first time since 1973, and 'Crazy Love' (from *Enlightened Rogues*) made an unexpected return to the set. Other highlights included Betts' solo song 'Good Times (Don't Fade Away)', 'Nobody Knows' (from *Shades of Two Worlds*), the powerful 'True Gravity', a cover of Chuck Willis' 'Feel So Bad', and a new instrumental called 'Rave On'. Duane Betts and Berry Oakley Jr. were guests on 'Dreams' on 10 and 11 March.

The album *Peakin' At The Beacon* selects mostly familiar tracks from the 2000 run – only 'Seven Turns' and an unexpected 'High Falls' post-date 1972. Derek Trucks' presence is immediately felt in a tracklist that favours the blues of 'It's Not My Cross to Bear', 'Every Hungry Woman', a sublime 'Please Call Home' and 'Leave My Blues at Home'. However, Warren Haynes' presence is sorely missed.

Tracklist:

1. 'Don't Want You No More', 2. 'It's Not My Cross To Bear', 3. 'Ain't Wastin' Time No More', 4. 'Every Hungry Woman', 5. 'Please Call Home', 6. 'Stand Back', 7. 'Black Hearted Woman', 8. 'Leave My Blues At Home', 9. 'Seven Turns', 10. 'High Falls'

David Fricke wrote in *Rolling Stone* in March 2001:

The Allmans remain a nightly wonder. In their middle age, they have evolved beyond band-dom into a great repertory orchestra – a rock equivalent of the Count Basie and Duke Ellington organizations, revisiting classic material with fresh, practised swing. All but two of the songs on Peakin' come from pre-'73 albums. Yet the Allmans still pull new suspense from the old standards: Betts' and Trucks' searing guitar harmonies, ascending in creeping-vine formation in the prolonged climax of 'Black Hearted Woman'; the greasy confidence of Trucks' slide break in 'Ain't Wastin' Time No More', and the way the last sustained note coolly drips into Gregg Allman's smoky voice. Peakin' is no replacement for the definitive thrills of 1971's *At Fillmore East*, but it presents the Allmans as a living thing with a sturdy song bag.

Sunday 7 May 2000, Atlanta, GA

By the time *Peakin' At The Beacon* was released, Dickey Betts had been fired from the band. His last gig was at the seventh annual Midtown Music Festival in Atlanta on 7 May 2000. Gregg Allman:

Dickey was drinking a ton of beer, and god-only-knows what else he was doing. He was in rare form, blowing song after song, and the worse he got, the louder he played. It was a total train wreck, and just embarrassing to the rest of us. As I walked off the stage, I had it in my mind that I was going to resign from The Allman Brothers Band. As it turns out, Butch was thinking the same thing, and told his wife Melinda and our manager Bert Holman that he would never play with Dickey Betts again. We got a conference call (9 May 2000) set up with Jaimoe, and he agreed that Dickey was out of control.

They were close to disbanding, as Gregg told *Hittin The Note* four years later: 'We were on our way home, and I had already mapped out my letter of resignation. And I think Butch had too. We got together and talked. We said, 'Hell, there is no reason why we should leave'. Butch asked me, 'Are you through with the Brothers?'. I said, 'No, I don't think I am'.

A few days later, Allman, Trucks, Jaimoe and manager Bert Holman discussed a plan. Gregg:

The three of us felt (Dickey) needed to get into rehab and that we should play the summer tour without him, but Jaimoe would not agree to saying he would never play with Dickey again. I remember Jaimoe saying something like, 'The only way out of The Allman Brothers Band is to quit or die'. It stuck with me, because Jaimoe was right – it was a brotherhood and those were the rules, and it speaks volumes about Jaimoe's character too after what Dickey had done to him back in 1980. But we agreed that we could not let Dickey's demons take away what we had worked so hard for. We decided to look for another guitar player to play the 2000 summer tour with us.

Allman, Trucks, Jaimoe and Holman sent a letter to Betts on 10 May 2000. Allman:

And then the shit hit the fan. In the years since then, Dickey has said that we fired him by fax. We never fired him; we said nothing about not working with him ever again. We chose our words carefully. What we told him was this: 'Dickey, we've been together a long time – we love you and respect you – but you're getting way off base here, and you're bringing your worldly crap onstage with you. It's been going on so long that we would like to inform you that this next year we're going to be playing with another guitar player, so you can go into rehab; go do whatever you need to do to get yourself fixed. Then hopefully, at the end of the year, we can get back together'. That is not firing him.

Betts phoned Allman: his bandmate for over 30 years. Allman recounted the call years later:

I said, 'Dickey, don't even start. I don't want to talk to you'. 'What the hell is this?' he asked. 'You're firing me out of my own band?'. 'Man, this ain't your band no more – you done pissed it away', I said. He kept going on and on, and I finally said, 'Dickey, I don't care to talk to you at all. You can talk to me through my attorney'. And that was the last time I spoke to Dickey Betts.

Press coverage was immediate. Jaan Uhelszki wrote in *Rolling Stone*, in 23 May 2000

Dickey Betts is not taking his suspension from the band, lying down. On May 20, Betts fired off a missive to the Allman Brothers' official website *www.allmanbrothersband.com*, explaining the content of the infamous fax sent to him last week telling him his services would no longer be needed: 'Last Thursday, I received a fax notifying me that I would not be performing this summer with ABB. It said, 'You have not been performing well, and our shows have been repeatedly disappointing to both us and our fans as a result'. The implication was that I was suffering from some sort of health or drug problem. THIS IS TOTALLY, ABSOLUTELY, UNFOUNDED!', wrote the guitarist.

And from Lori Reese in *Entertainment Weekly* in May 2000:

Betts tells us he received a fax last week informing him that the other band members had voted him off the summer tour. Betts says the fax implied he needs help with a substance abuse problem. 'It says, 'We hope that you will seek treatment and return to us happy and healthy in the fall', says the guitarist, reading from the fax. Betts strongly denies the accusation. Several years ago, he admits, 'I did have a problem. I did bow out for a while and I fully admit that I needed help. I was out of line. But not this time. That's why this is so confusing. I really don't understand what's gone wrong. We have no more drug problems in the band'. For that reason, he remains confused by the band's action, and has sought further explanation from other members. After receiving the fax, he says no one contacted him. So Betts phoned Allman, only to get a bewildering answer: 'I called Gregg, and he was very short with me. He said, 'If you don't know, I ain't going to tell you. Just listen to f-ing tapes'. I listened to those tapes and I thought they sounded pretty good!'.

Butch Trucks told *Rolling Stone*: 'Ain't no way we can fire Dickey. We will be doing the summer tour without him. I will not get into the details. I will not comment further about what is going on with Dickey. Do any of you remember a summer a few years ago (1993) when we had to tour without him?'.

Gregg Allman wrote:

Without Duane and without Berry, there needed to be a leader in the band, and the question that has been asked for years, is why didn't I take it? Well, the answer is, because the first thing I would've done is fire Dickey and get another guitar player; when I think of the time and money he wasted in the studio and during rehearsal. We must've been pretty attached as a band to take that crap from him for so long before we finally said, 'Hey, man, you're out of here'.

Dickey Betts' instrumental pieces 'In Memory Of Elizabeth Reed', 'Jessica' and 'Les Brers In A Minor' were retained in the band's setlist, but his signature song 'Ramblin' Man' would never again be performed by The Allman Brothers Band. It's perhaps ironic, therefore, that Betts' composition 'High Falls' (from *Peakin' at the Beacon*) was nominated as Best Rock Instrumental Performance at the 44th Grammy Awards in 2001.

Part IV: 16 June 2000-28 October 2014

Hittin' the Note (2003)

Personnel:
Gregg Allman: Hammond B3 organ, piano, clavinet, lead vocals
Oteil Burbridge: bass
Warren Haynes: lead, slide, acoustic and acoustic slide guitars, lead and background vocals
Jaimoe: drums
Marc Quiñones: percussion
Butch Trucks: drums
Derek Trucks: lead, slide, acoustic slide guitars
Recorded December 2001 and April 2002 at Water Music, Hoboken, NJ
Producers: Michael Barbiero, Warren Haynes
Release date: March 2003
Chart position: 37

Hittin' The Note is the band's 12th and final studio album. With Dickey Betts now firmly out of the picture (after May 2000, he never again appeared live or on record with the band), they looked for a permanent replacement. Betts was replaced for the rest of the year by Jimmy Herring: Oteil Burbridge's former bandmate from Aquarium Rescue Unit.

Reports of the summer 2000 dates with Herring were very favourable: a thrilling 'Loan Me A Dime' from the tour – with Herring in top form – was included in the *Trouble No More* box set. Derek Trucks said in 2009: 'It was hard for Jimmy to take the role of one of his musical idols. Jimmy was in a tough spot. There was a lot of heat on him. Jimmy has pretty thick skin, and he did it as well as anyone could. That year with Jimmy was essential to righting the ship'.

At the beginning of 2001, Warren Haynes was considering his options following Allen Woody's death the previous August. Haynes appeared as a 'special guest' with ABB at the One For Woody concert in September 2000, then at a benefit concert in December 2000, and again at the band's spring 2001 residency at the Beacon. With the Beacon shows established as a highlight of the band's year, in 2001, they premiered three new songs sung by Gregg – 'Desdemona', 'Who To Believe', and 'High Cost Of Low Living' – and also a new arrangement of Gov't Mule's 'Rockin' Horse', and a toothsome cover of Otis Redding's 'I've Been Loving You Too Long': both sung by Warren Haynes.

Haynes rejoined permanently for the 2001 summer tour. Gov't Mule was put on hold for three years, and The Allman Brothers Band settled as Allman, Burbridge, Haynes, Jaimoe, Quiñones, Trucks and Trucks. This lineup endured for more than 13 years, right through to October 2014. Haynes was very much the driving force of this longest-lasting, much-loved and – as it transpired – final lineup of the band. Derek Trucks said, 'When Warren came back, it was off to the races'.

Haynes co-wrote nine of the album's eleven songs, and co-produced the album with long-time associate Michael Barbiero. Tom Dowd's health was declining, and the legendary producer was unable to directly contribute to the sessions, though he was sent rough mixes, and provided feedback. Warren Haynes explained at the time:

This record has that classic Allman Brothers sound and feel. It also explores new territory without turning its back on the institution. That's a fine line that every band has to draw as they continue to grow: how far into a new direction can you do without diluting your signature sound? (*Hittin' The Note*) has the feeling of an album that really needed to be made, and it has turned out great. The vibe was just great, everybody was in a good space and we were all keen on getting it done. Everything fell into place, because it felt like everybody really wanted to be there.

Gregg Allman:

For the first time in as long as I could remember, we were a group who all liked each other. No more dictators, no more drunks. It was like it had been way back at the start all those years ago – an attitude that Butch, Jaimoe and I hadn't felt since Macon. On that record, we rekindled something that had been lost for so long – that feeling of what this band was really supposed to be about. The groove was back in the Allman Brothers.

Most of the album was recorded live in ten days at Water Music, Hoboken, in December 2001. Co-producer Michael Barbiero noted: 'Because everyone was playing in the room together, it turned out to be a very ambient and believable live performance. There are very few overdubs on the album: almost all of it is live'.

Track for track, *Hittin' The Note* might just be the band's strongest and most consistent studio release since *Idlewild South*. The tracks 'Old Before My Time', 'Maydell', 'Firing Line' and 'Instrumental Illness' were debuted at the band's March 2002 residency at the Beacon in New York City. They completed a 13-date run at the Beacon in 2003 to coincide with the album's release.

Gregg told John Lynskey in 2003: 'This record has brought a whole new breath of live into the band. We're talking about playing more dates, because this album deserves that kind of support. It's too good not to'.

Butch Trucks suggested: 'Sit back and enjoy yourself. This one was a long time in coming, but it's been worth the wait'.

'Firing Line' (Gregg Allman, Warren Haynes)
Released as a single, 2002. Chart position: 37 (US Mainstream)
Seriously funky, the attention-grabbing 'Firing Line' comes across as the bastard son of Stevie Wonder and Gov't Mule. Warren Haynes said, 'Gregg and I wrote

'Firing Line' together in New York a few days before we started rehearsing. I had written that little opening riff, and Gregg started playing a complimentary piano line'.

Man, it pops. Talk about setting out your stall.

'High Cost Of Low Living' (Gregg Allman, Warren Haynes, Jeff Anders, Ronnie Burgin)

This menacing but dynamic track is another classic song. Haynes:

'High Cost Of Low Living' goes back a long long way. It was started by a friend of mine, Ronnie Burgin. We were best of friends growing up, and together we learned how to play guitar. Ronnie had started that song, and I think it was called 'The High Cost Of Living Low'. He had taken it to our friend Jeff Anders, added more lyrics and had some groove ideas for it. Then Jeff brought it to me. By that time, Ronnie was dead, and Jeff thought it would be nice to finish the song for him. I took it a little further, but it still wasn't complete. I showed it to Gregg, and he came up with the bridge. That's what it really needed – that was the icing on the cake. So 'High Cost' was almost 15 years in the making.

Otiel's bubbling bass and that incomparable double-drum sound lay the foundation for a climbing dual guitar melody line and a spectacular Derek Trucks slide run. Gregg is magnificent – once again, his voice is a thing of majesty. Spectacular.

'Desdemona' (Gregg Allman, Warren Haynes)

'Desdemona' is a potent and compelling song – familiar in its 6/8 blues-based style but effortlessly powerful in delivery. Warren Haynes: '(It was) the first song Gregg and I wrote together when I went down to his place in Savannah. To me, 'Desdemona' really raised the bar for the entire project. That song is gorgeous – it has a Ray Charles quality to it that I love'.

As with 'Statesboro Blues', there's a waltz-time jam (starting at 2:56) that *should* sound ridiculous but somehow fits perfectly. Derek's playing is utterly sublime. The switch back from this section to the verse at 7:01 is as unexpected as it is remarkable. Bassist Oteil Burbridge noted: 'To me, that's the one song on the record that's up there with their first four or five. It's got a kind of timeless sound'.

'Woman Across The River' (Bettye Crutcher, Allen Jones)

Warren Haynes sings this song made famous by bluesman Freddie King. Haynes said, 'I've heard a bunch of different versions of Freddie doing it, but we just kind of made it our own'.

Marc Quiñones: '('Woman Across The River') goes from the funk to the shuffle, and then back to funk – it's a great song to play because of all the things going on in it'.

'Old Before My Time' (Gregg Allman, Warren Haynes)

An outstanding song, brilliantly sung and beautifully produced. Gregg: 'Old Before My Time' is a very personal song. I've been through some pretty tough times in my life. Butch really loved that song – he felt it was me at my absolute best, which was nice of him to say'.

Initially written by Gregg on acoustic guitar, Warren Haynes shaped the structure, and also (re)wrote the lyric based on Allman's initial ideas. The slide solo is by Warren: 'It was the one song I wanted to play the slide solo on'.

Derek Trucks adds beautiful melodic round-toned slide-guitar fills, complementing Gregg's jaded vocal.

'Who to Believe' (Warren Haynes, John Jaworowicz)

Another older song, first brought to the band in the mid-1990s. It was written with John Jaworowicz, who is also credited on 'End Of The Line' from *Shades Of Two Worlds*.

It's an attractive funky blues, with the Warren Haynes stamp, and an Allman-friendly bad-woman lyric. From 3:30 to 4:34, Derek Trucks gives a master class in slide guitar control and mood.

'Maydell' (Warren Haynes, Johnny Neel)

The album's one misstep, 'Maydell' is rather too close to 'Trouble No More' and 'Good Clean Fun'. It's the album's shortest track, and might've been better utilised as a B-side.

'Rockin' Horse' (Gregg Allman, Warren Haynes, Allen Woody, Jack Pearson)

ABB first recorded this during sessions for *Where It All Begins*. Evidently, both 'Soulshine' and 'Rockin' Horse' were laid down without Dickey Betts, who'd decided to go home. The band left space for his guitar to be added when he returned to the studio. 'Soulshine' was completed, but Betts chose not to work on 'Rockin' Horse'. That 1994 version remains unreleased.

'Rockin' Horse' was reworked as a Gov't Mule song, and they played it as early as 1994. It returned to ABB's live set in March 2001 and stayed there for almost 250 performances as a guitar/vocal showcase for Warren Haynes. Haynes said, 'When we started playing 'Rockin' Horse' with The Allman Brothers Band, it opened new doors to that song. All of a sudden there's this great big band for what used to be a trio song'.

The song was road-hardened by the time sessions for *Hittin' The Note* rolled around. It was recorded several times, but the first take was the one selected.

'Heart Of Stone' (Mick Jagger, Keith Richards)

This Rolling Stones song was part of ABB's setlist as early as 1995. Slowed down and souled out, think of The Stones covered by Albert King. It seems somehow perfect for Gregg, who sings brilliantly. Derek shines, as always. Astonishing, really.

'Instrumental Illness' (Warren Haynes, Oteil Burbridge)

A 12-minute mix of funk, jazz and rock, the musically complex and highly original 'Instrumental Illness' gives a rare songwriting credit to Oteil Burbridge. Marc Quiñones told *Hittin The Note* in 2001: 'Haynes and Oteil just sat there and came up with the melody. Everybody's energy is so positive right now that they were able to write that song in a day or two'.

The pulsating bass line brings to mind a jazz-funk arrangement of 'Whipping Post', and the shimmering guitars imitate horn lines. Hammond organ – compete with a short punchy solo – anchors the patent ABB swinging drum shuffle, before Derek's sublime slide guitar takes the lead. The band builds-in a wonderfully dynamic section powered by percussion, leading to a long section featuring Haynes' funk-blues guitar. 'Instrumental Illness' shares the same DNA as 'In Memory Of Elizabeth Reed', 'Les Brers In A Minor', 'High Falls' and 'True Gravity', but follows a different evolutionary path. It sits alongside those enduring classics. Burbridge demurs: 'It's not as involved as something like 'High Falls', because we wanted to put more into the jams rather than into the form of the song. It packs the same punch, it's just that the focus is a little more shifted'.

'Instrumental Illness' was nominated for Best Rock Instrumental Performance at the 46th Annual Grammy Awards in 2003.

'Old Friend' (Warren Haynes, Chris Anderson)

This was first recorded by American roots-blues musician Chris Anderson (formerly one of many members of perpetual support act Outlaws) for his 1995 solo album of the same name. Warren Haynes' driving slide guitar is unmistakable on that version.

The stripped-down version here is just Haynes and Derek Trucks, both playing acoustic slide guitar (Trucks' is a dobro). Haynes said, 'The sound of those two guitars, blends perfectly. It's almost like one big instrument, and I think it was the right way to finish off the album'.

It is perhaps ironic that the last song on the last album by ABB does not feature any of the musicians from the band's first 20 years. But then again, Haynes and Trucks were such hugely important components of this final iteration, that it's highly appropriate that *these* two men close the door on the Allman Brothers Band's long and varied studio career.

> You know hard time is just an old friend to me
> Tell me now, old friend, when you gonna let me be?

One Way Out: Live at the Beacon Theatre (2004)

Personnel:
Gregg Allman: Hammond B3 organ, piano, acoustic guitar, lead vocals
Oteil Burbridge: bass
Warren Haynes: lead and slide guitars, lead and background vocals
Jaimoe: drums
Marc Quiñones: percussion, background vocals
Butch Trucks: drums
Derek Trucks: lead and slide guitars
Recorded March 2003 at the Beacon Theatre, New York
Producers: Michael Barbiero, Warren Haynes
Release date: March 2004
Chart position: 190

> The best live album of their career, because both age and youth suit them, and because they're better now than they ever were.
> **Robert Christgau, 2004**

Do we really need a sixth Allman Brothers' live album? Well, yes. *One Way Out: Live at the Beacon Theatre* showcases the energy and control of the rejuvenated band, as recorded during their 2003 residency in New York. As well as the classics 'Statesboro Blues', 'Don't Keep Me Wonderin'', 'Midnight Rider', 'Trouble No More', 'Wasted Words' (back in the set for the first time since 1975), 'Ain't Wastin' Time No More', an incredible 'Come And Go Blues', 'Every Hungry Woman', 'Dreams' (with Haynes on lead guitar) and 'Whipping Post', there was room for a mighty live version of the more recent 'Rockin' Horse' (segueing into an astounding 'Desdemona': an intense and astonishing 23 minutes of music), the expansive 'Instrumental Illness', and top-class renditions of 'Old Before My Time', 'High Cost Of Low Living' and 'Woman Across The River'. There's also the first release for the band's cover of Sonny Boy Williamson's 'Good Morning Little School Girl', along with a version of 'Worried Down With The Blues' from Gov't Mule's 2001 album *The Deepest End*, which had included Allman and Burbridge as guests. Burbridge said, 'I like that one because it's so slow. There's so much space in it'.

Here is a band most definitely not resting on their laurels churning out tired sets of their greatest hits. To the surprise of many, the band often ended their set with 'Layla' on this tour: in recognition of producer Tom Dowd who died the previous October. There was no room for that track on *One Way Out*, but it featured on the band's next live album.

'Instrumental Illness' was nominated for the Grammy for Best Rock Instrumental Performance in 2004.

The DVD *Live At The Beacon Theatre* followed in September 2003. This comprises three hours of music recorded over 25 and 26 March 2003 (Trucks plays lead on 'Dreams'), and 78 minutes of interviews and backstage footage.

Tracklist
Disc One:
1. 'Statesboro Blues', 2. 'Don't Keep Me Wonderin'', 3. 'Midnight Rider', 4. 'Rockin' Horse', 5. 'Desdemona', 6. 'Trouble No More', 7. 'Wasted Words', 8. 'Good Morning Little School Girl', 9. 'Instrumental Illness'

Disc Two:
1. 'Ain't Wastin' Time No More', 2. 'Come And Go Blues', 3. 'Woman Across The River', 4. 'Old Before My Time', 5. 'Every Hungry Woman', 6. 'High Cost Of Low Living', 7. 'Worried Down With The Blues', 8. 'Dreams', 9.'Whipping Post'

The Fox Box (2004)

Personnel:
Gregg Allman: Hammond B3 organ, piano, acoustic guitar, vocals
Oteil Burbridge: bass, vocals
Warren Haynes: guitar, vocals
Jaimoe: drums
Marc Quiñones: percussion, vocals
Butch Trucks: drums
Derek Trucks: guitar
Jack Pearson: guitar ('Dreams' (24 September)), 'Mountain Jam' reprise',
'Southbound'
Susan Tedeschi: guitar, vocals ('Don't Think Twice, It's All Right')
Vaylor Trucks: guitar 'One Way Out'
Rob Barraco: keyboards ('The Same Thing', 'In Memory Of Elizabeth Reed')
Recorded September 2004 at The Fox Theatre, Atlanta, Georgia
Producers: The Allman Brothers Band
Release date: 2004.
Chart position: did not chart

After the last few dates of the 2003 summer tour, the band agreed to release instant live albums of their shows on their own Peach Records label, in an arrangement with Clear Channel Entertainment. 100 live shows would be released between 2004 and 2007.
A new deal with Munck Music resulted in the Peach Records release of over 200 live Allman Brothers Band albums between April 2007 and October 2014, just about every concert they gave in this period. These are also available as a series of *Complete Set* compilations, and are for the most-rabid collectors only. These were generally soundboard mixes without any remixing.

However, in 2004 and 2009, the band released professionally mixed sets of shows from Atlanta and New York. *The Fox Box* documents three complete concerts over three nights at Atlanta's Fox Theatre: 24-26 September 2004. Astoundingly, they played 50 different songs across these three shows. Only 'Dreams' was played more than once, and featured different soloists on each version.

Highlights include Gregg's impeccable first vocal performance of 'Blue Sky'; an unexpected medley of Derek and the Dominos' 'Why Does Love Got To Be So Sad?' and Grateful Dead's 'Franklin's Tower' with Oteil on lead vocals; 'Black Hearted Woman', extending to 30 minutes; returning guest, guitarist Jack Pearson's sublime and graceful slide solo on the first night's 'Dreams'; Howlin' Wolf's 'Who's Been Talkin''; 'Layla' (simply phenomenal); 40 minutes of 'Liz Reed'; a frenetic 'The Same Thing', and Susan Tedeschi singing Dylan.

Despite its hefty price tag, the nine-CD box sold out its initial 2004 run before being re-released in 2005 and again in 2017.

Tracklist
Disc one – September 24, 2004
1. 'Mountain Jam', 2. 'Trouble No More', 3. 'Midnight Rider', 4. 'Wasted Words', 5. 'Worried Down With The Blues', 6. 'You Don't Love Me', 7. 'Ain't Wastin' Time No More'
Disc two:
1. 'Rockin' Horse', 2. 'Hot 'Lanta', 3. 'Melissa', 4. 'Come And Go Blues', 5. 'Can't Lose What You Never Had', 6. 'Why Does Love Got To Be So Sad?', 7. 'Franklin's Tower'
Disc Three:
1. 'Black Hearted Woman', 2. 'Dreams' (Jack Pearson solo), 3. 'Mountain Jam' reprise, 4. 'Southbound'
Disc Four – September 25, 2004
1. 'Les Brers In A Minor (Intro)', 2. 'Don't Want You No More'/'It's Not My Cross To Bear', 3. 'Statesboro Blues', 4. 'Stand Back', 5. 'Who's Been Talking', 6. 'Soulshine', 7. 'Good Clean Fun', 8. 'Old Before My Time', 9. 'Woman Across The River', 10. 'Instrumental Illness'
Disc Five:
1. 'The Night They Drove Old Dixie Down', 2. 'Leave My Blues At Home', 3. 'Key To The Highway', 4. 'Don't Think Twice, It's All Right', 5. 'One Way Out', 6. 'Blue Sky', 7. 'Dreams' (Derek Trucks solo), 8. 'Les Brers In A Minor', 9. 'Layla'
Disc Six – September 26, 2004:
1. 'Revival', 2. 'Every Hungry Woman', 3. 'Done Somebody Wrong', 4. 'Hoochie Coochie Man', 5. 'Desdemona', 6. 'High Cost Of Low Living', 7. '44 Blues', 8. 'End Of The Line'
Disc Seven:
1. 'Dreams' (Warren Haynes solo), 2. 'I Walk On Gilded Splinters', 3. 'Stormy Monday', 4. 'The Same Thing', 5. 'In Memory Of Elizabeth Reed'
Disc Eight:
1. 'In Memory Of Elizabeth Reed' continued, 2. 'Don't Keep Me Wonderin'', 3. 'No One To Run With', 4. 'Whipping Post'

Mention should be made here of the 2007 album *Warren Haynes Presents The Benefit Concert Volume 2*, which was recorded on 21 December 2000 at the Thomas Wolfe Auditorium in Asheville, North Carolina. It features otherwise unavailable live performances of 'Ain't Wastin Time No More', 'Born Under A Bad Sign', 'Soulshine', 'Statesboro Blues' (Jimmy Herring replaces an unavailable Derek Trucks), and Warren and Gregg singing 'Come And Go Blues'.

Wednesday 19 December 2007, Macon, GA

On 19 December 2007, The Allman Brothers Band gained their own museum: The Big House in Macon, Georgia.

The band's post-1989 revival had initiated the simple black-and-white 16-page newsletter *Hittin' The Note*. This succeeded an earlier newsletter called *Les Brers*, which shipped nine issues from winter 1985 to spring 1988. In 1992, the band's long-term friend and archivist Kirk West founded *Hittin' The Note* with Bill Ector, Joe Bell and editor Ron Currens. In time, the newsletter gained a professional footing with full-time employees, and expanded to a 60-page (later 80-page) colour magazine, with wide distribution. Working closely with the band and their managers, the *HTN* team established merchandise lines and very much acted as the public face of the band. Across 85 quarterly editions, *Hittin' The Note* played a major role in the Allman Brothers' success over their final couple of decades.

Since 1973, The Big House had changed hands many times: including spells as a beauty parlour and lawyer's office. It was slowly falling into disrepair when Kirk and Kirsten West bought it in 1993. 2321 Vineville was established as the HQ of *Hittin' The Note* and the band's merchandise arm Kid Glove Productions. There were also a couple of museum rooms housing the West's extensive collection of ABB memorabilia: an estimated 300,000 pieces. The Wests decided to sell up in 2003, and the house and contents were put up for sale. The following spring, the Big House Foundation was formed as a non-profit organisation to raise funds to buy the house and preserve the home and history of the band. The overall fundraising goal was $4,000,000, to cover the purchase of the house, conversion to a museum, and future upkeep. Fans could donate $100 and receive a t-shirt or spend a little bit more for a personally-engraved brick or CD display.

The band their management fully supported the venture. On 22 March 2005, one of the band's regular dates at New York's Beacon Theatre was given over to a Big House fundraiser. This seven-hour concert included sets by ABB (with Chuck Leavell), Gov't Mule, The Derek Trucks Band, Oteil's Peacemakers and Jaimoe's Jasssz Band.

Kirk West's 2007 documentary *Please Call Home* served as a further fundraiser for the museum, as did the sterling work of the Georgia Allman Brothers Band Association.

The Big House Museum opened in November 2009, joining a growing list of museums dedicated to singers and bands, including Cavern Mecca (Liverpool, opened in 1981), Elvis' Graceland (Memphis, 1982), The Bob Marley Museum (Kingston, Jamaica, 1987), The Beatles' Story (Liverpool, 1990), Shania Twain (Timmins, 2001), The Ramones (Berlin, 2005) and many since. It's manned by volunteers, and has a small permanent staff. Gregg Allman:

> Now we even have a museum of the Brothers' history set up at the Big House in Macon, which I think is wonderful. One of our long-time tour personnel

came up with the idea of turning the house into a museum. All the guys in the band got behind it, and we reached out to some of our friends and fans and asked them to help fund it, because it takes a lot of money to keep that thing up: to keep it clean, keep all the photos. We had to put an air system in there so that things wouldn't wrinkle up. You don't want the stuff to look shopworn and all yellowed out. Of course, you need a good sound system – all that stuff. And I'll be damned if it didn't work. The museum makes me real real proud, and I try to get down there as much as I can.

The Beacon Box (2009)

Personnel:
Gregg Allman: organ, lead vocals
Oteil Burbridge: bass
Warren Haynes: guitar, vocals
Jaimoe, Butch Trucks: drums
Marc Quiñones: percussion
Derek Trucks: guitar
With:
Devon Allman, Trey Anastasio, John Bell, Scott Boyer, Larry Campbell, Eric Clapton, Billy Gibbons, John Hammond, Boz Scaggs, Susan Tedeschi, Bob Weir, Johnny Winter: guitar, vocals
Chris Anderson, John Berry, Randy Brecker, Mark Pender: trumpet
Joe Bellia, James van de Bogert, Adam Nussbaum, Bernard Purdie, Paul Riddle, Lenny White: drums
Becca Bramlett, Bonnie Bramlett, Sheryl Crow, Ruthie Foster, Mike Mattison, Floyd Miles, Kid Rock, Southside Johnny, Teresa Williams: vocals
Stanley Clarke, Jerry Jemmott, John Paul Jones, Berry Oakley Jr., Tal Wilkenfeld: bass
Phil Lesh: bass, vocals
Roosevelt Collier, Robert Randolph: pedal steel guitar
Karl Denson: saxophone
Ron Holloway, Joey Stann: tenor saxophone
Eddie Manion: baritone saxophone
Richie 'La Bamba' Rosenberg: trombone
Thom Doucette, John Popper, Bruce Willis: harmonica
JJ Grey, Jimmy Hall, Taj Mahal: harmonica, vocals
Robben Ford, Buddy Guy, Jimmy Herring, David Hidalgo, Sonny Landreth, Bob Margolin, Cesar Rojas, Tommy Talton: guitar
Levon Helm: drums, vocals
Bruce Hornsby, Page McConnell, Brian Mitchell, Jimmy Smith: keyboards
Bruce Katz, Chuck Leavell, Danny Louis, Ivan Neville: piano
Recorded 9-28 March 2009 at the Beacon Theatre, New York; 12 December 2008 at Asheville, NC
Producers: The Allman Brothers Band
Release date: 2009
Chart positions: did not chart

This 47-disc box set (yes, 47) comprises every gig performed in the band's spring 2009 residency at the Beacon in New York. Over these 16 concerts, more than 60 guest musicians joined the band to perform over 100 songs in celebration of the band's 40th anniversary.

9 March 2009 includes a set of ABB rarities, including 'I Walk On Gilded Splinters', 'The Same Thing' and 'Leaving Trunk'; a second set featuring

Taj Mahal (including his 'Statesboro Blues' which the band had played for decades), and three songs originally by The Band: with guests Levon Helm, Larry Campbell and Teresa Williams. Long versions of 'Black Hearted Woman' and 'Mountain Jam', close the set.

10 March 2009 saw the band invite Johnny Winter onstage for three scintillating blues songs. Cesar Rojas and David Hidalgo from Los Lobos also join for an immense 'Good Morning Little School Girl'. 12 March 2009 features Buddy Guy singing 'The Sky Is Crying' and 'You Don't Love Me'. Two members of Phish – Trey Anastasio and Page McConnell – play on lengthy workouts of 'I Know You Rider' and 'In Memory Of Elizabeth Reed'. The following night debuted a five-piece horn section, and Bruce Willis on harmonica. Boz Scaggs sings a scintillating 'Loan Me A Dime' and two other songs. On the 14th, Randy Brecker (trumpet), Robert Randolph (pedal steel) and Stanley Clarke (bass) add to a jam-heavy set which includes Miles Davis' 'In A Silent Way', Led Zeppelin's 'Dazed And Confused', and extended versions of ABB's 'Rockin' Horse', 'Gambler's Roll', 'Revival', 'Woman Across The River', 'Dreams', 'In Memory Of Elizabeth Reed' and 'Mountain Jam'.

John Hammond, Bonnie Bramlett, Becca Bramlett and Susan Tedeschi were guests on 16 March 2009. The band perform a rare version of Gregg's solo song 'Oncoming Traffic', and a 30-minute 'Jessica' closes the show. The next night, Scott Boyer and Tommy Talton (from Capricorn labelmates Cowboy) sing three songs, as does Missouri-born chanteuse Sheryl Crow.

Eric Clapton joined for the second set of each show on 19 and 20 March 2009: his first live shows with ABB. Clapton performed five songs from his Derek and the Dominos period – 'Key To The Highway', 'Why Does Love Got To Be So Sad?', 'Little Wing', 'Anyday' and 'Layla'. He also sat in for the Allman Brothers classics 'Stormy Monday', 'Dreams' and 'In Memory Of Elizabeth Reed'.

Derek Trucks reflected on Clapton's startling guitar solo in the 15-minute version of 'In Memory Of Elizabeth Reed': 'That was a different side of him that I hadn't seen. Where he normally would've gotten to his point – stayed and got out – he got in, stayed and realised he wasn't nearly finished. He kept ploughing. There was a freedom and unhinged element to it that I really dug'.

The horn section is present once more on 21 March 2009, beefing up 'The Same Thing', 'Soulshine' and 'Little By Little', and colouring several songs sung by Susan Tedeschi. Bruce Hornsby plays piano on the whole of the second set.

Two nights later, the band was joined by legendary session players Jerry Jemmott (bass), Bernard Purdie (drums) and Jimmy Smith (keyboards), who between them have played on thousands of songs. Vocals on 'Soul Serenade', 'Memphis Soul Stew' and 'Them Changes' were by Mike Mattison of The Tedeschi Trucks Band. The second set included contributions from two members of Widespread Panic: guitarist Jimmy Herring (who replaced Dickey Betts in ABB in 2000) and vocalist John Bell. ABB also played a new unnamed instrumental, which sits comfortably alongside their previous long jazz-infused pieces.

Sonny Landreth added his own distinctive slide guitar-playing to several songs during the first set on 24 March. The same night, ZZ Top's Billy Gibbons powered through 'Statesboro Blues' and 'Stormy Monday' and his own 'Jesus Just Left Chicago'. In a bluesy evening, Bob Margolin (1970s Muddy Waters guitarist) sang two songs, and the band hosted harmonica maestros Thom Doucette (long-time guest with ABB) and Blues Traveler's John Popper. Popper was also a member of Frogwings in 1999, with Butch Trucks, Derek Trucks, Marc Quinones and Oteil Burbridge.

There were no guests on 26 March – the band simply performed their first two albums from top to bottom, on the 40th anniversary of the band's formation.

The next-to-last show of the run included performances with Jimmy Hall of Wet Willie and Betts, Hall, Leavell and Trucks; keyboardist Ivan Neville, and Kid Rock. Devon Allman (son of Gregg), Berry Oakley Jr. and Hall lead the band through a bluesy 'The Sky Is Crying' and two Wet Willie numbers. Kid Rock sings 'Soulshine' and a cover of the Marshall Tucker Band classic 'Can't You See', which also featured original MTB drummer Paul Riddle. The Allman Brothers Band – alarmingly – played 'Freebird'.

Finally, the last concert recorded on 28 March 2009 has considerable contributions from the band's former pianist Chuck Leavell. Leavell has toured with The Rolling Stones for 40 years, and played on the best-selling live album of all time: Eric Clapton's *Unplugged*. The band's old friend Floyd Miles (who jammed with Duane and Gregg in Daytona Beach in the 1960s) sings 'Born Under A Bad Sign' and 'Stormy Monday Blues', and the Grateful Dead's Phil Lesh and Bob Weir appear for nearly an hour of 'Sugaree', 'I Know You Rider' and 'Franklin's Tower'. An extended 'Rockin' Horse' and a Haynes/Trucks/ Burbridge performance of 'Little Martha' are highlights of this three-hour show. Warren Haynes:

I thought it was the best Beacon run so far. The band played great, and all of the guests were outstanding. It was almost a surreal experience. Levon Helm and Taj Mahal set the tone on the first night, and they raised the bar pretty high for everybody else. Buddy Guy was great, and I thought it was a cool thing for Trey and Page from Phish to come out that night: that was an extremely diverse juxtaposition of sets. Los Lobos were wonderful. Johnny Winter was great. Billy Gibbons was amazing. Bonnie and Bekka Bramlett were full of energy. Playing with Eric (Clapton) was a huge personal highlight. It was a nice opportunity for him to enter a different world. From night to night, guest to guest, it just went great.

The Beacon Box came in a hefty wood case with a glossy booklet, souvenir backstage passes and a two-CD bonus show from December 2008. The price was a cool $499.99. It's worth every penny.

The band continued to fill the Beacon Theatre each year, also touring through the summer – the Haynes/Trucks front line were never less than magnificent, and Gregg Allman was in good voice. However, he struggled with health issues, as his rock-and-roll lifestyle started to catch up with him. He was diagnosed with hepatitis C in 2007, and three tumours were discovered in his liver the following year. He underwent a successful liver transplant in 2010, as his seventh solo album *Low Country Blues* gave him his highest-ever solo chart placing. Lung surgery and rehab in 2012 allowed time for Allman to complete and publish his frank memoir *My Cross to Bear*.

The album and DVD *All My Friends: Celebrating the Songs & Voice of Gregg Allman* documents a January 2014 concert at the Fox Theatre in Atlanta. This 26-song recording and video showcases Allman's rich legacy. Warren Haynes and Derek Trucks open the show with 'Come And Go Blues' and 'End Of The Line', and there are terrific performances by Susan Tedeschi, Sam Moore, Keb' Mo', Taj Mahal (singing 'Statesboro Blues'), Dr. John, John Hiatt, Jackson Browne (duetting with Gregg on 'These Days' and 'Melissa'), Widespread Panic with ex-ABB guitarist Jimmy Herring, Trace Adkins, Martina McBride, Vince Gill, Zac Brown and Eric Church. The Allman Brothers Band wrap up the show with – perhaps predictably – 11 minutes of 'Dreams' and 13 of 'Whipping Post'. This entire show is worthy of your attention.

Tuesday, 28 October 2014

The Allman Brothers Band retired after the last concert of their October 2014 season at the Beacon Theatre. Since spring 1969, they'd logged in-excess of 2,300 concert appearances.

Derek Trucks said, 'I feel that the Tedeschi Trucks Band is where my future and creative energy lies. The tour schedule keeps growing, and I feel the time has finally come to focus on a single project, which will allow me to spend that rare time off the road with my family and children. It's a difficult decision to make, and I don't make it lightly'.

The setlist for their final bow concentrated on the band's 1969-1972 successes, playing almost every song from their first four albums.

Set I:
'Little Martha', 'Mountain Jam', 'Don't Want You No More/It's Not My Cross to Bear', 'One Way Out', 'Good Morning Little School Girl', 'Midnight Rider', 'The High Cost Of Low Living', 'Hot 'Lanta', 'Blue Sky', 'You Don't Love Me'

Set II:
'Statesboro Blues', 'Ain't Wastin' Time No More', 'Black Hearted Woman', 'The Sky Is Crying', 'Dreams', 'Don't Keep Me Wonderin'', 'In Memory Of Elizabeth Reed'

Set III:
'Melissa', 'Revival', 'Southbound', 'Mountain Jam/Will the Circle Be Unbroken?/ Mountain Jam'

Encore:
'Whipping Post', 'Trouble No More'

Butch Trucks said at the time: 'It's a very emotional time right now. It was such a huge part of my life, especially when I was in the band, but even prior to that. That music means more to me than anyone could imagine. Being on the inside of it and helping keep it alive, was an unbelievable experience'.

To the end, they were 'hittin' the note', as Trucks explained:

Hittin' the note is reaching that point where you can't do any wrong. With us, when we're playing music, it's where the brain goes away and the body just does what it's supposed to do, and there's no thought and there's no question, and no matter what you do, it's right. It's getting to that spiritual level where the communication is total, but it's not mental. Spirituality has to be there, or it isn't music. I greatly adhere to the philosophy that what makes us human is that we have a brain and that we need to use it. And we need to not take too much on faith, and we should always be questioning and rational and thinking. Once you quit doing that, you're not human anymore. Then you're like some kind of cattle. What's happened with the great religions and the wars of the world, tends to show that to be true. But something happens when you're playing music, that kind of bypasses the brain and just goes straight to something else. Now, you have to use your brain to get it going. In order to play what we play, you know, there's thought, there's a lot of thought. But once it gets going – once that spark is lit – then everything starts flowing and there's this unity, this spirituality, this communication that happens, and that's when you're hittin' the note.

Retrospective Live Albums

Since 2002, ABB have released a series of vintage live recordings – mostly from 1970-1973, but some from more recent shows. The earliest of these is *Bear's Sonic Journals: Fillmore East, February 1970* (2018), recorded 11-14 February 1970 at the Fillmore East in New York City. The Allman Brothers were on a bill with the Grateful Dead, and their renowned soundman Owsley 'Bear' Stanley recorded incomplete Allman Brothers sets over 11, 13 and 14 February. These were first released in 1996 as a mix of the three shows, with some tracks edited in from different performances. The 2018 release includes a remaster of the 1996 release, along with all available recordings from the three concerts – including the earliest-available versions of 'In Memory Of Elizabeth Reed' (the opening track in each set), and a long workout on Little Milton's 'I'm Gonna Move To The Outskirts Of Town'. The performances and fidelity are excellent.

Live at the Atlanta International Pop Festival: July 3 & 5, 1970* (2003) was recorded in Byron, Georgia. This two-CD set is curiously mixed with vocals prominent and drums way back, but the performances are stellar, despite it replicating much of *At Fillmore East*.

American University 12/13/70 (2002) is sourced from a concert in Washington, D.C.. The mix is boomy and not quite as interesting as other live recordings from the period, even if Duane's playing is magnificent.

Recordings from 1971 include the massive *Fillmore West '71* (2019) recorded over the three nights of 29-31 January 1971 in San Francisco, two months before the more-famous *At Fillmore East*. These are tightly-performed full concert recordings, but again with a mix that's clearly been restored from very old tapes. A bonus 'Mountain Jam' here is from the Warehouse in New Orleans, 13 March 1970. *Boston Common, 8/17/71* (2007) covers much the same ground as the Fillmore East full concert recordings. *Live from A&R Studios* (2016) was recorded before a small audience in New York on 26 August 1971. The show was broadcast live over WPLJ FM, and had been available on bootleg for years.

Three shows from the last few weeks of Duane Allman's life, are available – *S.U.N.Y. at Stonybrook: Stonybrook, NY 9/19/71* (2003), *Down in Texas '71* (2021), recorded 28 September 1971 at the Austin Municipal Auditorium, and *The Final Note* (2020), recorded 17 October 1971 at the Painters Mill Music Fair in Owings Mills, Maryland. 'Blue Sky' makes its debut at the first of these shows, which otherwise follow the band's standard set of the time. *The Final Note* includes songs from the band's last concert with Duane Allman, captured on a handheld cassette recorder.

The 1972-1973 era is represented by *Macon City Auditorium: 2/11/72* (2004) and *Nassau Coliseum, Uniondale, NY: 5/1/73* (2005). The Macon concert took place just weeks after Duane Allman's death and immediately before the release of *Eat a Peach*. This is the only official recording of the five-piece band. By the following year – with Lamar Williams and Chuck Leavell adding a more-jazz-like sensibility, the Nassau concert records the band at the peak of their commercial success. Seven songs exceed ten minutes' duration; the final three total 70 minutes!

Play All Night: Live at the Beacon Theatre 1992 (2014) documents two mighty shows from a ten-night run at the band's latter-day home-from-home. These were recorded for a potential live album, and some performances from these dates are included on *An Evening with the Allman Brothers Band: First Set* (1992). The Betts/Haynes partnership is in full flow here. *Cream of the Crop 2003* (2018) is a four-CD, 36-song set from various full concert recordings in July and August 2003. The revitalised post-Betts band stretch out on 33 minutes of 'In Memory Of Elizabeth Reed' in Pittsburgh, and more than 40 of 'Mountain Jam' in Charlotte. Warren Haynes told *Billboard* in 2018: 'It was a really good time period for the band. We had all the new material, and we were reinventing a lot of old material, and the band was on a high note at that point, so it just seemed like a good thing to go back and make available to folks'.

Finally, a magnificent show from July 2005 is available as *Warner Theatre, Erie, PA 7-19-05* (2020). This is late-period Allman Brothers Band at their best. A fluid 'Jessica' with astounding Trucks/Haynes interplay, complements newer songs from *Hittin' The Note* such as 'Firing Line' and 'The High Cost Of Low Living', and an in-concert favourite called 'JaMaBuBu': a long piece featuring the band's three drummer/percussionists and bassist Oteil Burbridge. Essential.

The grey market of re-released radio broadcasts has seen CDs of concerts from 1971, 1972, 1976, 1979, 1986, 1989 (all recorded in New York City) and 1994 (Holmdel, NJ).

Epilogue: The Road Goes On Forever

After the final Allman Brothers Band shows, Gregg Allman kept busy touring with his own band, and in 2015 released the live album *Gregg Allman Live: Back to Macon, GA*. However, his health problems remained – atrial fibrillation and a return of his liver cancer necessitated the cancellation of several shows in 2015 and 2016.

Fellow founder-member Butch Trucks formed his Freight Train Band, which originally included Berry Oakley Jr. on bass, and Butch's son Vaylor on guitar. In this same period (2016-2017), Trucks, Jaimoe, Quiñones, Burbridge and other musicians, including Lamar Williams Jr. and former ABB-guitarist Jack Pearson, toured as Les Brers. Both bands played selections from ABB's extensive back catalogue. Warren Haynes appeared with Les Brers on occasion. Haynes continues to record and perform with Gov't Mule, with ten studio albums, two solo albums and hundreds of full concert recordings to his credit.

Derek Trucks led his Derek Trucks Band from 1994 to 2010, with bassist Todd Smallie, drummer Yonrico Scott, keyboardist Kofi Burbridge (Oteil's brother) and, later, vocalist Mike Mattinson. The Derek Trucks Band released six studio albums. The 2003 album *Soul Serenade* includes his astonishing arrangement of the King Curtis track of the same name, and a guest appearance from Gregg Allman on a soulful version of Ray Charles' 'Drown In My Own Tears'.

Trucks toured extensively as a member of Eric Clapton's band in 2006/2007. In 2010, Trucks formed the highly-regarded Tedeschi Trucks Band with the Burbridge brothers, Mike Mattinson, and Trucks' wife: guitarist/vocalist Susan Tedeschi. They've released five studio albums, and sometimes add Allman Brothers songs such as 'Don't Keep Me Wonderin'', 'In Memory Of Elizabeth Reed', 'Dreams' and 'Whipping Post' to their lengthy live sets. Their annual touring schedule includes a residency at New York's Beacon Theatre: continuing the tradition set by the Allman Brothers from 1989. Trucks – a remarkably talented musician – has twice appeared on *Rolling Stone*'s list of The 100 Greatest Guitarists of All Time.

Oteil Burbridge plays in Dead & Company with ex-Grateful Dead members Mickey Hart, Bill Kreutzmann and Bob Weir, and also plays with his own trio. Marc Quiñones is a busy session player and tours with The Doobie Brothers.

Any future plans for an ABB reunion were definitively settled with the deaths of Gregg Allman and Butch Trucks in 2017 – the only two musicians to play in every variant of the Allman Brothers Band from March 1969 to October 2014.

Trucks died by his own hand, on 24 January 2017. Gregg Allman said, 'I'm heartbroken. I've lost another brother, and it hurts beyond words'. Les Brers played their final concert in honour of Trucks at the Wanee Festival in Florida on 20 April 2017. Five weeks later, Gregg died of liver cancer, despite having undergone a liver transplant in 2010. He was recording a solo album *Southern Blood* at Muscle Shoals that was posthumously released later in 2017. A proposed tour had been cancelled due to his health issues. He wrote: 'If I fell over dead right now, I have led some kind of life. I wouldn't trade it for nobody's, but I don't know if I'd do it again. If somebody offered me a second round, I think I'd have to pass on it'. Singer Sheryl Crow said he 'sounded like he'd already lived a thousand lifetimes'.

Gregg Allman and Butch Trucks are buried at Roseville cemetery in Macon, Georgia, close to the graves of Berry Oakley and Duane Allman.

Only Jaimoe and Dickey Betts now survive from the original 1969-1971 lineup. Betts suffered a mild stroke in 2018 and had to cancel several tour dates. He slipped and hit his head soon after. Successful surgery followed, but he has now retired – his last concert date was at the Peach Festival in Scranton, PA, on 22 July 2018. In 2019, Betts released the live album *Ramblin' Man Live at the St. George Theatre*.

Jaimoe has played in Jaimoe's Jasssz Band with the talented vocalist/ guitarist Junior Mack since 2005. Their live set combines aspects of R&B with freewheeling jazz and jam song structures, and includes a generous dose of Allman Brothers classics. Their sole studio album *Renaissance Man* (2012) includes a tough and funky version of 'Melissa' that is every inch as good as the Allmans' original. Jaimoe has recently recorded three albums as part of the J & F Band with Joe Fonda: *From The Roots to the Sky* (2018), *Cajun Blue* (2020) and *Me and the Devil* (2021).

Butch Trucks' kids Vaylor and Melody perform vintage ABB material in their band Brother and Sister. Meanwhile, Gregg Allman's first son Michael (born in 1966) has his own band and released the albums *Hard Labor Creek* (2009) and *Blues Travels Fast* (2006). Gregg's son with Cher – Elijah Blue, born in 1976 – is the lead singer of heavy metal band Deadsy, who have released five albums. Gregg's second daughter Layla Brooklyn Allman (born 1993) was the lead singer of Picture Me Broken, who released the album *Wide Awake* in 2010. Allman's son Devon (born in 1972) founded the band Honeytribe in 1999, recorded and toured with the Royal Southern Brotherhood between 2011 and 2014, and released the solo albums *Turquoise* (2013), *Ragged & Dirty* (2014) and *Ride or Die* (2016). He now performs with Betts' son Duane and Berry Oakley Jr. as The Allman Betts Band. Their debut album *Down To The River*, was recorded at Muscle Shoals Sound Studios and released in 2019. In concert, they play classic Allman Brothers and Gregg Allman tunes, such as 'Don't Keep Me Wonderin'', 'Dreams', 'Blue Sky', 'Melissa', 'I'm No Angel', 'Multi-Coloured Lady' and 'Midnight Rider'. Their second album, *Bless Your Heart* came out in 2020.

That same year saw the five-CD Allman Brothers Band career retrospective *Trouble No More: 50th Anniversary Collection*. All of the band's 13 lineups are represented. Unlike the *Dreams* box, there is no room here for pre-ABB or solo music. Disc one and the first half of disc two cover the Duane Allman period of 1969-1971. They include an alternative studio take of 'Trouble No More', the scintillating career-high version of 'You Don't Love Me/Soul Serenade' from the A&R broadcast. The remainder of disc two includes familiar tracks from *Brothers And Sisters*. Disc three extends from 1973 to 1981, as the band moved from Capricorn to Arista. It includes an unreleased 'Mountain Jam' from

Watkins Glen. The decade from 1990 to 2000 covers the band's albums *Seven Turns, Shades Of Two Worlds* and *Where It All Begins,* with the unreleased track 'I'm Not Cryin'' recorded live at the Beacon in 1999 with Jack Pearson on lead vocals. Finally, disc five includes two tracks from *Hittin' The Note,* and a generous seven unreleased live performances from 2000-2014. The band sings 'Loan Me A Dime': a semi-regular in 2000. This includes a jaw-dropping solo from Jimmy Herring: the only officially-released performance from his tenure with the band. Gregg sings an immense 'Blue Sky' in 2005, with a beautiful Derek Trucks slide solo and a guest appearance by the band's former pianist Chuck Leavell. The collection concludes with a second 'Trouble No More': the last encore from the band's last-ever concert.

The *Trouble No More* box set was promoted with a one-off show at Madison Square Garden, New York, on 10 March 2020. All of the remaining members of the final Allman Brothers Band lineup were present and correct – guitarists Derek Trucks and Warren Haynes, bassist Oteil Burbridge, drummer Jaimoe and percussionist Marc Quinones. Derek's younger brother Duane held down his Uncle Butch's old post on drums. Reese Wynans filled Gregg's role on organ. Wynans, you'll recall, was a member of the pre-Allman band Second Coming, and was part of the 1969 jam session from which The Allman Brothers Band was founded.

After a few days of rehearsals at SIR in Chelsea, 'The Brothers' – as they were billed – kicked off a three-and-a-half-hour concert with the opening salvo from the band's debut album: 'Don't Want You No More'/'It's Not My Cross To Bear'. Lead vocals were handled by Warren Haynes. 'Statesboro Blues', 'Revival', 'Trouble No More', 'Don't Keep Me Wonderin'' and 'Black Hearted Woman' preceded 'Dreams' and the instrumental 'Hot 'Lanta'. Chuck Leavell joined for 'Come And Go Blues', the awesome 'Soulshine', 'Stand Back' and 'Jessica', to conclude a thrilling first set.

The second set started with 'Mountain Jam', with Derek effortlessly and superbly playing Duane Allman's 1957 Gibson Les Paul (which sold at auction for $1,025,000 in 2019), then 'Blue Sky' with Chuck on lead vocals, a stupendous 'Desdemona', then 'Ain't Wasting Time No More', 'Every Hungry Woman', 'Melissa' 'In Memory Of Elizabeth Reed', 'No One To Run With' and 'One Way Out'. Encores of 'Midnight Rider' and 'Whipping Post' concluded a very strong performance, utterly dominated by the astounding talent of Derek Trucks, who is every inch the equal of Duane Allman in his prime.

Warren Haynes – present for 30 of the band's 50 years – said, 'What a great way to honour the music and fulfil that wish (of a final show) at the same time'.

There is a long hard road
It lies so far behind me...
'Old Before My Time', The Allman Brothers Band (2003)

Bibliography

Alan, P., *One Way Out: The Inside History of the Allman Brothers Band* (St. Martin's Press, New York City, 2014)

Allman, G., *Please Be With Me: A Song For My Father Duane Allman* (Random House, New York City, 2014)

Allman, G, with Light, A., *My Cross To Bear* (William Morrow, New York City, 2012)

Altschuler, G., *All Shook Up: How Rock 'n' Roll Changed America* (Oxford University Press, Oxford, 2005)

Beatty, B., *'You Wanna Play In My Band, You'd Better Come To Pick': Duane Allman And American Music* (Middle Tennessee State University, 2018)

Beatty, B., *Play All Night! Duane Allman And The Journey To Fillmore East* (University Press of Florida, Gainesville, 2022)

Clapton, E., *Eric Clapton – The Autobiography* (Arrow, Stratford-upon-Avon, 2008)

Christgau, R., *Christgau's Record Guide: Rock Albums of the Seventies* (Vermilion and Company, London, 1982)

Crowe, C., *The Day The Music Died* (Plexus Publishing Limited, Medford, 1989)

Davis, C. with DeCurtis, A., *The Soundtrack of My Life* (Simon & Schuster, New York, 2013)

DeCurtis, A. and Henke, J. (eds), *The Rolling Stone Album Guide: Revised Edition* (Virgin Books, London, 1992)

Freeman, S., *Midnight Riders: The Story of the Allman Brothers Band* (Little, Brown and Company, London, 1996)

Gilmore, M., *Night Beat: A Shadow History of Rock 'n' Roll* (Anchor, New York, 1999)

Greenfield, R., *The Last Sultan: The Life and Times of Ahmet Ertegun* (Simon & Schuster, New York, 2011)

Lynskey, J. (ed.), *Hittin' The Note: The Quarterly Almanac for Allman Brothers Band Fans* #17, 25, 27-28, 31, 35-76 (Kid Glove Enterprises, Macon, 1997-2013)

Lynskey, J., *50 Years, Five Decades, Half a Century* (line notes to *Trouble No More* box set, 2019)

Marsh, D. and Swenson, J. (eds), *The Rolling Stone Album Guide* (Virgin Books, London, 1980)

Myers, M., *Anatomy of a Song* (Grove Press, New York City, 2016)

Perkins, W., *No Saints, No Saviors: My Years with the Allman Brothers Band* (Mercer University Press, Macon, 2005)

Perkins, W. and Weston, J, *The Allman Brothers Band Classic Memorabilia 1969-1976* (Mercer University Press, Macon, 2015)

Poe, R., *Skydog: The Duane Allman Story* (Hal Leonard Corporation, Milwaukee, 2006)

Walden, A. with Feinberg, S., *Southern Man: Music and Mayhem in the American South* (Jawbone Press, London, 2021)